PREFACE TO SECOND EDITION

THE earlier edition of this book having been
out of print now for some years, advantage
has been taken of the opportunity created
by the constant request for its reprint to
incorporate some 50 pages additional matter
(including one complete chapter) collected
in the intervening decade.

DUDLEY WRIGHT.

1st September 1924.

PREFACE TO FIRST EDITION

THE awakened interest in supernormal
phenomena which has taken place in recent
years has included in its wake the absorbing
subject of Vampirism. Yet there has not
been any collection published of vampire
stories which are common to all the five
continents of the globe. The subject of

vampirism is regarded more seriously to-
day than it was even a decade since, and
an attempt has been made in this volume
to supply as far as possible all the instances
which could be collected from the various
countries. How far a certain amount of
scientific truth may underlie even what
may be regarded as the most extravagant
stories must necessarily be, for the present,
at any rate, an open question ; but he would
indeed be a bold man who would permit
his scepticism as to the objective existence
of vampires in the past or the possibility
of vampirism in the future to extend to
a categorical denial. If this collection of
stories helps, even in a slight degree, to the
elucidation of the problem, the book will
not have been written in vain.

DUDLEY WRIGHT.

1st September 1914.

CONTENTS

VAMPIRES AND VAMPIRISM

VAMPIRES AND VAMPIRISM

LEGENDS FROM AROUND THE WORLD

By DUDLEY WRIGHT

Lethe
PRESS

Immerse yourself in forgotten works

First published in 1914, revised edition 1924
by William Rider and Son, Ltd, this paperback edition
is first published in 2001 by Lethe Press

ISBN 1-59021-002-6

Manufactured in the United States of America

Lethe 102 Heritage Avenue, Maple Shade, NJ 08052
P R E S S lethepress@aol.com

VAMPIRES AND VAMPIRISM

CHAPTER I

INTRODUCTORY

WHAT is a vampire ? The definition given in Webster's *International Dictionary* is: " A blood-sucking ghost or re-animated body of a dead person ; a soul or re-animated body of a dead person believed to come from the grave and wander about by night sucking the blood of persons asleep, causing their death."

Whitney's *Century Dictionary* says that a vampire is : " A kind of spectral body which, according to a superstition existing among the Slavic and other races on the Lower Danube, leaves the grave during the night and maintains a semblance of life by sucking the warm blood of living men and women while they are asleep.

1   1

Dead wizards, werwolves, heretics, and
other outcasts become vampires, as do also
the illegitimate offspring of parents themselves illegitimate, and anyone killed by
a vampire."

According to the *Encyclopædia Britannica* :
" The persons who turn vampires are generally wizards, suicides, and those who come
to a violent end or have been cursed by
their parents or by the Church. But anyone may become a vampire if an animal
(especially a cat) leaps over the corpse or
a bird flies over it."

Among the specialists, the writers upon
vampire lore and legend, two definitions
may be quoted :—Hurst, who says that :
" A vampyr is a dead body which continues
to live in the grave ; which it leaves, however, by night, for the purpose of sucking
the blood of the living, whereby it is
nourished and preserved in good condition,
instead of becoming decomposed like other
dead bodies " ; and Scoffern, who wrote :
" The best definition I can give of a vampire
is a living mischievous and murderous dead
body. A living dead body ! The words
are idle, contradictory, incomprehensible,
but so are vampires."

Hence a corpse being held in a tightly sealed room before burial.

"Vampires," says the learned Zopfius, "come out of their graves in the night time, rush upon people sleeping in their beds, suck out all their blood and destroy them. They attack men, women, and children, sparing neither age nor sex. Those who are under the malignity of their influence complain of suffocation and a total deficiency of spirits, after which they soon expire. Some of them being asked at the point of death what is the matter with them, their answer is that such persons lately dead rise to torment them."

Not all vampires, however, are, or were, suckers of blood. Some, according to the records, despatched their victims by inflicting upon them contagious diseases, or strangling them without drawing blood, or causing their speedy or retarded death by various other means.

Messrs Skeat and Blagden, in *Pagan Races of the Malay Peninsula* (vol. i. p. 473), state that "a vampire, according to the view of Sakai of Perak, is not a demon—even though it is incidentally so-called—but a being of flesh and blood," and support this view by the statement that the vampire cannot pass through walls and hedges.

The word *vampire* (Dutch, *vampyr* ;
Polish, *wampior* or *upior* ; Slownik, *upir* ;
Ukraine, *upeer*) is held by Skeat to be
derived from the Servian *wampira*. The
Russians, Morlacchians, inhabitants of
Montenegro, Bohemians, Servians, Arnauts,
both of Hydra and Albania, know the
vampire under the name of *wukodalak,
vurkulaka,* or *vrykolaka,* a word which
means "wolf-fairy," and is thought by some
to be derived from the Greek. In Crete,
where Slavonic influence has not been felt,
the vampire is known by the name of
katakhaná. Vampire lore is, in general,
confined to stories of resuscitated corpses
of male human beings, though amongst the
Malays a *penangglan,* or vampire, is a living
witch, who can be killed if she can be
caught in the act of witchery. She is
especially feared in houses where a birth
has taken place, and it is the custom to
hang up a bunch of thistle in order to catch
her. She is said to keep vinegar at home
to aid her in re-entering her own body. In
the Malay Peninsula, parts of Polynesia and
the neighbouring districts, the vampire is
conceived as a head with entrails attached,
which comes forth to suck the blood of

living human beings. In Transylvania, the belief prevails that every person killed by a *nosferatu* (vampire) becomes in turn a vampire, and will continue to suck the blood of other innocent people until the evil spirit has been exorcised, either by opening the grave of the suspected person and driving a stake through the corpse, or firing a pistol-shot into the coffin. In very obstinate cases it is further recommended to cut off the head, fill the mouth with garlic, and then replace the head in its proper place in the coffin ; or else to extract the heart and burn it, and strew the ashes over the grave.

or put the ashes of the Vampire in water & have victims drink.

The *murony* of the Wallachians not only sucks blood, but also possesses the power of assuming a variety of shapes, as, for instance, those of a cat, dog, flea, or spider ; in consequence of which the ordinary evidence of death caused by the attack of a vampire, viz. the mark of a bite in the back of the neck, is not considered indispensable. The Wallachians have a very great fear of sudden death, greater perhaps than any other people, for they attribute sudden death to the attack of a vampire, and believe that anyone destroyed by a vampire must

Instead of the side of the neck like most modern depictions.

become a vampire, and that no power can save him from this fate. A similar belief obtains in Northern Albania, where it is also held that a wandering spirit has power to enter the body of any individual guilty of undetected crime, and that such obsession forms part of his punishment.

Some writers have ascribed the origin of the belief in vampires to Greek Christianity, but there are traces of the superstition and belief at a considerably earlier date than this. In the opinion of the anthropologist Tylor, " the shortest way of treating the belief is to refer it directly to the principles of savage animism. We shall see that most of its details fall into their places at once, and that vampires are not mere creations of groundless fancy, but causes conceived in spiritual form to account for specific facts of wasting disease." It is more than probable that the practice of offering up living animals as sacrifices to satisfy the thirst of departed human beings, combined with the ideas of the Platonist and the teachings of the learned Jew, Isaac Arbanel, who maintained that before the soul can be loosed from the fetters of the flesh it must lie some months with it in the grave, may have influenced the belief and assisted its development. Vampirism found a place in Babylonian belief and in the folk-lore and traditions of many countries of the Near East. The belief was quite common in Arabia, although there is no trace of it there in pre-Christian times. The earliest references to vampires are found in Chaldean and Assyrian tablets. Later, the pagan Romans gave their adherence to the belief that the dead bodies of certain people could be allured from their graves by sorcerers, unless the bodies had actually undergone decomposition, and that the only means of effectually preventing such " resurrections " was by cremating the remains. In Grecian lore there are many wonderful stories of the dead rising from their graves and feasting upon the blood of the young and beautiful. From Greece and Rome the superstition spread throughout Austria, Hungary, Lorraine, Poland, Roumania, Iceland, and even to the British Isles, reaching its height in the period from 1723 to 1735, when a vampire fever or epidemic broke out in the south-east of Europe, particularly in Hungary and Servia. The belief in vampires even spread to Africa, where the

Kaffirs held that bad men alone live a second time and try to kill the living by night. According to a local superstition of the Lesbians, the unquiet ghost of the Virgin Gello used to haunt their island, and was supposed to cause the deaths of young children.

Various devices have been resorted to in different countries at the time of burial, in the belief that the dead could thus be prevented from returning to earth-life. In some instances, *e.g.* among the Wallachians, a long nail was driven through the skull of the corpse, and the thorny stem of a wild rose-bush laid upon the body, in order that its shroud might become entangled with it, should it attempt to rise. The Kroats and Slavonians burned the straw upon which the suspected body lay. They then locked up all the cats and dogs, for if these animals stepped over the corpse it would assuredly return as a vampire and suck the blood of the village folk. Many held that to drive a white thorn stake through the dead body rendered the vampire harmless, and the peasants of Bukowina still retain the practice of driving an ash stake through the breasts of suicides and supposed vampires—

much like what Vlades Jepés did to emissaries from Turkey.

Bram Stoker might be influenced by this change in law.

a practice common in England, so far as suicides were concerned, until 1823, when there was passed " An Act to alter and amend the law relating to the interment of the remains of any person found *felo de se*," in which it was enacted that the coroner or other officer " shall give directions for the private interment of the remains of such person *felo de se* without any stake being driven through the body of such person." It was also ordained that the burial was only to take place between nine and twelve o'clock at night.

The driving of a stake through the body does not seem to have had always the desired effect. De Schartz, in his *Magia Postuma*, published at Olmutz in 1706, tells of a shepherd in the village of Blow, near Kadam, in Bohemia, who made several appearances after his death and called certain persons, who never failed to die within eight days of such call. The peasants of Blow took up the body and fixed it to the ground by means of a stake driven through the corpse. The man, when in that condition, told them that they were very good to give him a stick with which he could defend himself against the dogs

smart-alec vampire!

which worried him. Notwithstanding the
stake, he got up again that same night,
alarmed many people, and, presumably
out of revenge, strangled more people in that
one night than he had ever done on a single
occasion before. It was decided to hand
over his body to the public executioner,
who was ordered to see that the remains
were burned outside the village. When
the executioner and his assistants attempted
to move the corpse for that purpose, it
howled like a madman, and moved its feet
and hands as though it were alive. They
then pierced the body through with stakes,
but he again uttered loud cries and a great
quantity of bright vermilion blood flowed
from him. The cremation, however, put
an end to the apparition and haunting of
the spectre. De Schartz says that the
only remedy for these apparitions is to cut
off the heads and burn the bodies of those
who come back to haunt their former
abodes. It was, however, customary to
hold a public inquiry and examination of
witnesses before proceeding to the burning
of a body, and if, upon examination of
the body, it was found that the corpse had
begun to decompose, that the limbs were

not supple and mobile, and the blood not fluidic, then burning was not commanded. Even in the case of suspected persons an interval of six to seven weeks was always allowed to lapse before the grave was opened in order to ascertain whether the flesh had decayed and the limbs lost their suppleness and mobility. A Strigon or Indian vampire, who was transfixed with a sharp thorn cudgel, near Larbach, in 1672, pulled it out of his body and flung it back contemptuously.

Bartholin, in *de Causa contemptûs mortis*, tells the story of a man, named Harpye, who ordered his wife to bury him exactly at the kitchen door, in order that he might see what went on in the house. The woman executed her commission, and soon after his death he appeared to several people in the neighbourhood, killed people while they were engaged in their occupations, and played so many mischievous pranks that the inhabitants began to move away from the village. At last a man named Olaus Pa took courage and ran at the spectre with a lance, which he drove into the apparition. The spectre instantly vanished, taking the spear with it. Next morning

Olaus had the grave of Harpye opened, when he found the lance in the dead body, which had not become corrupted. The corpse was then taken from the grave, burned, and the ashes thrown into the sea, and the spectre did not afterwards trouble the inhabitants.

To cross the arms of the corpse, or to place a cross or crucifix upon the grave, or to bury a suspected corpse at the junction of four cross-roads, was, in some parts, regarded as an efficacious preventive of vampirism. It will be remembered that it was at one time the practice in England to bury suicides at the four cross-roads. If a vampire should make its appearance, it could be prevented from ever appearing again by forcing it to take the oath not to do so, if the words " by my winding-sheet " were incorporated in the oath.

One charm employed by the Wallachians to prevent a person becoming a vampire was to rub the body in certain parts with the lard of a pig killed on St Ignatius's Day.

In Poland and Russia, vampires make their appearance from noon to midnight instead of between nightfall and dawn, the rule that generally prevails. They come and suck the blood of living men and animals in such abundance that sometimes it flows from them at the nose and ears, and occasionally in such profusion that the corpse swims in the blood thus oozing from it as it lies in the coffin. One may become immune from the attacks of vampires by mixing this blood with flour and making bread from the mixture, a portion of which must be eaten; otherwise the charm will not work. The Californians held that the mere breaking of the spine of the corpse was sufficient to prevent its return as a vampire. Sometimes heavy stones were piled on the grave to keep the ghost within, a practice to which Frazer traces the origin of funeral cairns and tombstones. Two resolutions of the Sorbonne, passed between 1700 and 1710, prohibited the cutting off of the heads and the maiming of the bodies of persons supposed to be vampires.

In the German folk-tale known as *Faithful John*, the statue said to the king : " If you, with your own hand, cut off the heads of both your children and sprinkle me with their blood, I shall be brought to life again." According to primitive ideas, blood is life, and to receive blood is to receive life : the soul of the dead wants to live, and, consequently, loves blood. The shades in Hades are eager to drink the blood of Odysseus's sacrifice, that their life may be renewed for a time. It is of the greatest importance that the soul should get what it desires, as, if not satisfied, it might come and attack the living. It is possible that the bodily mutilations which to this day accompany funerals among some peoples have their origin in the belief that the departed spirit is refreshed by the blood thus spilt. The Samoans called it an "offering of blood" for the dead when the mourners beat their heads till the blood ran.

The Australian native sorcerers are said to acquire their magical influence by eating human flesh, but this is done once only in a lifetime. According to Nider's *Formicarius*, part of the ceremony of initiation into wizardry and witchcraft consisted in drinking in a church, before the commencement of Mass, from a flask filled with blood taken from the corpses of murdered infants.

The methods employed for the detection of vampires have varied according to the countries in which the belief in their existence was maintained. In some places it was held that, if there were discovered in a grave two or three or more holes about the size of a man's finger, it would almost certainly follow that a body with all the marks of vampirism would be discovered within the grave. The Wallachians employed a rather elaborate method of divination. They were in the habit of choosing a boy young enough to make it certain that he was innocent of any impurity. He was then placed on an absolutely black and unmutilated horse which had never stumbled. The horse was then made to ride about the cemetery and pass over all the graves. If the horse refused to pass over any grave, even in spite of repeated blows, that grave was believed to shelter a vampire. Their records state that when such a grave was opened it was generally found to contain a corpse as fat and handsome as that of a full-blooded man quietly sleeping. The finest vermilion blood would flow from the throat when cut, and this was held to be the blood he had sucked from the veins of living people. It is said that the attacks of the vampire generally ceased on this being done.

In the town of Perlepe, between Monastru and Kiuprili, there existed the extraordinary phenomenon of a number of families who were regarded as being the offspring of *vrykolakas*, and as possessing the power of laying the wandering spirits to which they were related. They are said to have kept their art very dark and to have practised it in secret, but their fame was so widely spread that persons in need of such deliverance were accustomed to send for them from other cities. In ordinary life and intercourse they were avoided by all the inhabitants.

Although some writers have contended that no vampire has yet been caught in the act of vampirism, and that, as no museum of natural history has secured a specimen, the whole of the stories concerning vampires may be regarded as mythical, others have held firmly to a belief in their existence and inimical power. Dr Pierart, in *La Revue Spiritualiste* (vol. iv. p. 104), wrote : " After a crowd of facts of vampirism so often proved, shall we say that there are no more to be had, and that these never had a foundation? Nothing comes of nothing. Every belief, every custom, springs from facts and causes which give it birth. If one had never seen appear in the bosom of their families, in various countries, beings clothed in the appearance of departed ones known to them, sucking the blood of one or more persons, and if the deaths of the victims had not followed after such apparitions, the disinterment of corpses would not have taken place, and there would never have been the attestation of the otherwise incredible fact of persons buried for several years being found with the body soft and flexible, the eyes wide open, the complexion rosy, the mouth and nose full of blood, and the blood flowing fully when the body was struck or wounded or the head cut off."

Bishop d'Avranches Huet wrote : " I will not examine whether the facts of vampirism, which are constantly being reported, are true, or the fruit of a popular error ; but it is beyond doubt that they are testified to by so many able and trustworthy authors, and by so many *eye-witnesses*, that no one ought

2

Greek / Russian
/ Orthodoxy
Catholicism is inherently
tied to European belief

to decide the question without a good deal
of caution."

Dr Pierart gave the following explanation of their existence : " Poor, dead
cataleptics, buried as if really dead in cold
and dry spots where morbid causes are incapable of effecting the destruction of their
bodies, the astral spirit, enveloping itself
with a fluidic ethereal body, is prompted
to quit the precincts of its tomb and to
exercise on living bodies acts peculiar to
physical life, especially that of nutrition,
the result of which, by a mysterious link
between soul and body which spiritualistic
science will some day explain, is forwarded
to the material body lying still within its
tomb, and the latter is thus helped to per-
petuate its vital existence."

Apart from the spectre vampire there is,
of course, the vampire bat in the world
of natural history, which is said to suck
blood from a sleeping person, insinuating
its tongue into a vein, but without inflicting pain. Captain Steadman, during his
expedition to Surinam, awoke early one
morning and was alarmed to find his
hammock steeped almost through and himself weltering in blood, although he was

without pain. It was discovered that he had been bitten by a vampire bat. Pennant says that in some parts of America they destroyed all the cattle introduced by the missionaries.

CHAPTER II

EXCOMMUNICATION AND ITS POWER

THE Greek Church at one time taught that
the bodies of persons upon whom the ban
of excommunication had been passed did
not undergo decomposition after death
until such sentence had been revoked by
the pronouncement of absolution over the
remains, and that, while the bodies remained in this uncorrupted condition, the
spirits of the individuals wandered up and
down the earth seeking sustenance from
the blood of the living. The non-corrup-
tion of a body, however, was also held to
be one of the proofs of sanctity; but, in
this case, the body preserved its natural
colour and gave an agreeable odour, whereas
the bodies of the excommunicated generally turned black, swelled out like a drum,
and emitted an offensive smell. Very frequently, however, when the graves of

suspected vampires were opened, the faces were found to be of ruddy complexion and the veins distended with blood, which, when opened with a lancet, yielded a supply of blood as plentiful, fresh, and free as that found in the veins of young and healthy living human beings. For many centuries in the history of Greek Christianity there was scarcely a village that had not its own local vampire stories which were related by the inhabitants and vouched for by them as having either occurred within their own knowledge or been related to them by their parents or relatives as having come within their personal observation or been verified by them.

The bodies of murderers and suicides were also held to be exempt from the law of dissolution of the mortal remains until the Church granted release from the curse entailed upon them by such act. The priests, by this assumption of power over the body as well as over the soul, made profitable use of this superstitious belief by preying upon the fears and credulity of the living. They also included in this ecclesiastical law of exemption from corruption after death those who in their lives had been guilty of heinous sins, those who had tampered with the magic arts, and all who had been cursed during life by their parents. These were all said to become vampires. This belief spread to other branches of the Christian Church, and the story is related that St Libentius, Archbishop of Bremen, who died 4th January 1013, once excommunicated a gang of pirates, one of whom died shortly afterwards and was buried in Norway. Seventy years afterwards his body was found quite entire and uncorrupted, nor did it fall to ashes until it had received absolution from the Bishop Alvareda.

Leo Allatius, a Roman Catholic, describes a corpse which he found in an undecomposed condition. He implies that the Greeks connected the circumstance with the power invested in them by the text : " Whatsoever thou shalt bind on earth shall be bound in heaven," and by which they hold that the soul is excluded from all hope of participation in future bliss so long as the body remains undecomposed. Poqueville, another writer, also states that whenever a bishop or priest excommunicated a person he added to the general sentence of excommunication the words : " After death, let not thy body have power to dissolve."

A manuscript was discovered many years ago in the Church of St Sophia at Thessalonica, which is an interesting commentary upon the power claimed by the Church over excommunicated bodies. The manuscript states that :

(1) Whoever has been laid under any curse or received any injunction from his deceased parents that he has not fulfilled, after his death the forepart of his body remains entire;

(2) Whoever has been the object of any anathema appears yellow after death, and the fingers are shrivelled ;

(3) Whoever appears white has been excommunicated by the divine laws ;

(4) Whoever appears black has been excommunicated by a bishop.

It was held possible to discover, by means of these signs, the crime for which, as well as the person on whom, the judgment had been pronounced. One horrible result of this ghastly superstition was the custom which was at one time prevalent among the Greeks of Salonica, as well as the Bulgarians in the centre of European

Turkey, and other nations, of disinterring indiscriminately the bodies of the dead after they had been buried for twelve months, in order to ascertain from the condition of the remains whether the souls were in heaven or hell, or perambulating the neighbourhood as vampires.

This assumed ecclesiastical power acted occasionally, however, injuriously on the clergy themselves. There is on record one instance where a priest was killed in revenge for the death of a man whose illness was attributed to the sentence of excommunication that had been passed upon him. On another occasion a bishop of some diocese in Morea was robbed by a band of brigands as he was passing through a portion of the Maniate territory. When the deed was done the mountaineers bethought themselves that the bishop would, in all probability, excommunicate them as soon as he reached a place of safety. They saw no means of averting this, to them, dreadful calamity, except by the committal of a further and more heinous crime; and so they set out in pursuit of the unfortunate bishop, whom they eventually overtook and murdered.

It seems there is a legacy of such violence so there is antipathy on both sides the case.

Many years ago a Greek of Keramia complained to the Pasha of Khania that the papás of his village had excommunicated him and so been the indirect cause of his having been bewitched. The Pasha sent for the priest, threw him into prison, and only released him upon payment of a fine of 300 piastres.

During a local war a native of Theriso was taken ill : the cry went up : " It is an aphorismos." The papás was accused, reviled, and threatened with murder unless the curse was removed; but the man continued to get worse, and eventually died. So firm was the belief of everyone in the neighbourhood that the ban had caused the man's death that some of his companions regarded it as a duty to avenge his fate, and, in consequence, they sought out the priest and shot him.

At the beginning of the nineteenth century the Metropolitan of Larissa was informed that a papás had disinterred two bodies and thrown them into the Haliæmon on pretence of their being vrukólakas. Upon being summoned before the bishop the priest admitted the truth of the accusation, and justified his act by saying that a report had

been current that a large animal, accompanied with flames, had been seen to issue
from the grave in which these two bodies
had been buried. The bishop fined the
priest 250 piastres, and sent a proclamation
throughout the diocese that, in future,
similar offences would be punished with
double that fine and be accompanied with
loss of position.

Martin Crusius tells the following curious
story. There were about the court of
Mahomet II. a number of men learned in
Greek and Arabic literature, who had in-
vestigated a variety of points connected
with the Christian faith. They informed
the Sultan that the bodies of persons
excommunicated by the Greek clergy did
not decompose, and when he inquired
whether the effect of absolution was to
dissolve them, he was answered in the
affirmative. Upon this, he sent orders to
Maximus, the Patriarch of that period, to
produce a case by which the truth of the
statement might be tested. The Patriarch
convened his clergy in great trepidation,
and after long deliberation they ascertained
that a woman had been excommunicated
by the previous Patriarch for the commis-

sion of grievous sins. They ascertained the
whereabouts of her grave, and when they
had opened it they found that the corpse
was entire, but swollen out like a drum.
When the news of this reached the Sultan,
he despatched some of his officers to possess
themselves of the body, which they did,
and deposited it in a safe place. On an
appointed day the liturgy was said over
it and the Patriarch recited the absolution
in the presence of the officials.   As this was
being done—wonderful to relate !—the bones
were heard to rattle as they fell apart in the
coffin, and at the same time, the narrator
adds, the woman's soul was also freed from
the punishment to which it had been condemned. The courtiers at once ran and
informed the Sultan, who was astonished at
the miracle, and exclaimed : " Of a surety
the Christian religion is true." Calmet
also relates this story, and adds that the
body was found to be entirely black and
much swollen ; that it was placed in a
chest under the Emperor's seal, which chest
was not opened until three days after the
absolution had been pronounced, when the
body was seen to be reduced to ashes.

During the long war between the Christians and Mohammedans in the island of Crete, it became a matter of astonishment that ravages caused by vampires were no longer the subject of conversation. "How can it be, when the number of deaths is so great, that none of those that die become katakhanás?" was the question asked, to be met with the answer: "No one ever becomes a katakhaná if he dies in time of war."

Leo Allatius also relates that he was told by Athanasius, Metropolitan of Imbros, that, on one occasion, being earnestly entreated to pronounce the absolution over a number of corpses that had long remained undecomposed, he consented to do so, and before the recitation was concluded they all fell away into ashes.

Rycaut relates a similar occurrence, to which he appends the following remark: "This story I should not have judged worth relating, but that I heard it from the mouth of a grave person who says that his own eyes were witnesses thereof."

The Hydhræans (or Hydhrioks) say there used to be a great number of vampires in Hydhra, and that their present freedom is to be attributed solely to the exertions

What is the purpose of rolling stones?

of their bishop, who banished them all to Santoréhe, where, on the desert isle, they now exist in great numbers, wandering about, rolling stones down the slope towards the sea, " as may be heard by anyone who passes near, in a kaík, during the night."

Interesting case

At the second Council of Limoges, held in 1031, the Bishop of Cahors made the following statement : " A knight of my diocese being killed in a state of excommunication, I refused to comply with the request of his friends, who solicited me earnestly to give him absolution. My resolution was to make an example of him, in order to strike terror into others. Notwithstanding this, he was buried in a church dedicated to St Peter by some soldiers or knights without any ecclesiastical ceremony, without any leave, and without the assistance of any priest. The next morning his body was found out of the grave, perfectly entire, and without any token of its having been touched. The soldiers who buried him opened the grave and found nothing but the linen which had been wrapped about his body. They then buried him afresh and covered the grave with an enormous quantity of earth and stones. The next

[handwritten marginal note: Rising of a corpse because of being buried apostate or hallowed/consecrated ground]

day the corpse was found out of the grave again, and there were no symptoms of anyone having been at work. The same thing was repeated five times, and at last they buried him in unconsecrated ground, at a distance from the churchyard, when no further incident occurred."

Rycaut states that the following story was related to him with many asseverations of truth by a grave *Candive Kalois* called Sofronio, a preacher, and a person of no mean repute and learning at Smyrna.

"I knew," he said, "a certain person who, for some misdemeanours committed in the Morea, fled over to the Isle of Milo, where, though he escaped the hand of justice, he could not avoid the sentence of excommunication, from which he could no more fly than from the conviction of his own conscience, or the guilt which ever attended him ; for the fatal hour of his death being come, and the sentence of the Church not revoked, the body was carelessly and without solemnity interred in some retired and unfrequented place. In the meantime the relatives of the deceased were much afflicted and anxious for the sad estate of their dead friend, whilst the

peasants and islanders were every night
affrighted and disturbed with strange and
unusual apparitions, which they immediately concluded arose from the grave of the
accursed excommunicant, which, according
to their custom, they immediately opened,
when they found the body uncorrupted,
ruddy, and the veins replete with blood.
The coffin was furnished with grapes,
apples, and nuts, and such fruits as the
season afforded. Whereupon, consultation
being taken, the Kaloires resolved to make
use of the common remedy in those cases,
which was to cut and dismember the body
into several parts and to boil it in wine, as
the approved means of dislodging the evil
spirit and disposing the body to a dissolution. But the friends of the deceased,
being willing and desirous that the corpse
should rest in peace and some ease given
to the departed soul, obtained a reprieve
from the clergy, and hoped that for a sum
of money (they being persons of a competent
estate) a release might be purchased from
the excommunication under the hand of
the Patriarch. In this manner the corpse
was for a little while freed from dissection,
and letters thereupon sent to Constanti-

nople with this direction, That in case the Patriarch should condescend to take off the excommunication, that the day, hour, and minute that he signed the remission should be inserted in the document. And now the corpse was taken into the church (the country people not being willing it should remain in the field), and prayers and masses were daily said for its dissolution and the pardon of the offender ; when one day, after many prayers, supplications, and offerings (as this Sofrino attested to me with many protestations), and whilst he himself was heard performing divine service, on a sudden was heard a rumbling noise in the coffin of the dead party, to the fear and astonishment of all persons then present ; which when they had opened they found the body consumed and dissolved as far into its first principles of earth as if it had been several years interred. The hour and minute of this dissolution was immediately noted and precisely observed, which being compared with the date of the Patriarch's release when it was signed at Constantinople, it was found exactly to agree with that moment in which the body returned to its ashes."

In most countries the vampire was regarded as a night-wanderer, but resting in its grave on Friday night, so that the ceremony of absolution had to be performed on that night or during Saturday, because, if the spirit was out on its rambles when the ceremony took place, it was unavailing.

The Sfakians generally believe that the ravages committed by these night-wanderers used in former times to be far more frequent than they are at the present day, and that they have become comparatively rare solely in consequence of the increased zeal and skill possessed by members of the sacerdotal order.

Tournefort relates an entertaining story of a vampire that woefully annoyed the inhabitants of Myconi. Prayers, processions, stabbing with swords, sprinklings of holy water, and even pouring the latter in large quantities down the throat of the refractory *vroucolaca* were all tried in vain. An Albanian who chanced to be at Myconi objected to two of these remedies. It was no wonder the devil continued in, he said, for how could he possibly come through the holy water ? And as to swords, they were equally effectual in preventing his

exit, for their handles being crosses, he was
so much terrified that he dare not pass
them. To obviate the latter objection, he
recommended that Turkish scymetars
should be used. The scymetars were
accordingly put in requisition, but the per-
tinacious devil still retained his hold of the
corpse and played his pranks with as much
vigour as ever. At length, when all the
respectable inhabitants were packing up to
take flight to Syra or Tinos, an effectual
method of ousting the *vroucolaca* was
fortunately suggested. The body was committed to the flames on January 1st, 1701,
and the spirit being thus forcibly ejected
from its abode, was rendered incapable of
doing further mischief.

There is a story told of St Stanislaus
raising to life a man who had been dead for
three years, whom he called to life in order
that he might give evidence on the saint's
behalf in a court of justice. After having
given his evidence, the resuscitated man
returned quietly to his grave.

Not malicious corpse — deals with hagiography

CHAPTER III

THE belief in the vampire and ghoul was prevalent even in Babylon and Assyria, where it was maintained that the dead could appear again upon earth and seek sustenance from the living. The belief is, in all probability, linked up with the almost universal theory that transfused blood is necessary for revivification. Baths of human blood were anciently prescribed as a possible remedy for leprosy.

Mr R. Campbell Thompson, in his work *The Devils and Evil Spirits of Babylonia*, states that the *Ekimmu* or departed spirit was the soul of the dead person unable to rest, which wandered as a spectre over the earth. " If it found a luckless man who had wandered far from his fellows into haunted places, it fastened upon him, plaguing and tormenting him until such time as a priest should drive it away with exorcisms."

Mr Thompson also gives the translation of the following two tablets, which, it will be seen, contain references to this belief :—

> The gods which seize (upon man)
>   Have come forth from the grave ;
> The evil wind-gusts
>   Have come forth from the grave.

To demand the payment of rites and the pouring out
    of libations,
  They have come forth from the grave ;
All that is evil in their hosts, like a whirlwind,
  Hath come forth from the grave.

The evil Spirit, the evil Demon, the evil Ghost, the evil
    Devil,
From the earth have come forth ;
From the underworld unto the land they have come
    forth ;
In heaven they are unknown,
On earth they are not understood.
They neither stand nor sit
Nor eat nor drink.

INCANTATION

> Spirits that minish heaven and earth,
> That minish the land,
> Spirits that minish the land,
> Of giant strength,

Of giant strength and giant tread,
Demons (like) raging bulls, great ghosts,
Ghosts that break through all houses,
Demons that have no shame,
Seven are they !
Knowing no care,
They grind the land like corn ;
Knowing no mercy,
They rage against mankind :
They spill their blood like rain,
Devouring their flesh (and) sucking their veins.
Where the images of the gods are, there they quake
In the temple of Nabu, who fertiliseth the shoots of
    wheat.
They are demons full of violence
Ceaselessly devouring blood.
Invoke the ban against them,
That they no more return to this neighbourhood.
By Heaven be ye exorcised ! By Earth be ye exorcised !

Greek Christianity, as already stated, has been credited by many with the origin of the vampire belief, but this contention is hardly borne out by facts. The belief was undoubtedly developed greatly under the influence of the Greek Church, and utilised by the Greek priests as an additional power which they possessed over the people. It did not become prominent in Greece until after the establishment of Christianity, and there are many remarkable stories told of vampire apparitions among the Slavonic races bordering on Greece, as well as among the Arabians. In later times, Father Richard, a French Jesuit of the seventeenth century, went as a missionary to the Archipelago, and has left an account of the islands of Santerini in which he discourses at length upon the *bucolacs* or vampires of that district.

Some Greeks believe that the spectre which appears is not really the soul of the deceased, but an evil spirit which enters his body after the soul of the owner has been withdrawn. Thus Leo Allatius, in describing the belief, says : " The corpse is entered by a demon which is the source of ruin to unhappy men. For frequently emerging from the tomb in the form of that body and roaming about the city and other inhabited places, especially by night it betakes itself to any house it fancies, and, after knocking at the door, addresses one of the inmates in a loud tone. If the person answers he is done for : two days after that he dies. If he does not answer he is safe. In consequence of this, all the people in Chios, if anyone calls to them by night, never reply the first time ; for if a second call is given they know that it does not proceed from the *vrykolaka* but from someone else."

In the *Menées des Grecs* it is recorded that an ecclesiastic of Scheti, being excommunicated by his superior for some act of disobedience, quitted the desert and came to Alexandria, where he was apprehended by the governor of the city, stripped of his religious habit, and strongly solicited to sacrifice to the idols of the place. The man bravely resisted the temptation, and was tortured in several ways, till at last they cut off his head, and threw his body out of the city to be devoured by dogs. The next night it was carried away by the Christians, who, having embalmed it and wrapped it up in fine linen, interred it in an honourable part of the church with all the respect due to the remains of a martyr. But at the next celebration of the Mass, upon the deacons crying out aloud as usual, " Let the catechumens and all who do not communicate retire," his grave instantly opened and the martyr retired into the church porch. When Mass was over he came again of his own accord into the grave. Not long afterwards it was revealed by an angel to a holy person, who had continued three days in prayer, that the deceased ecclesiastic had been excommunicated by his superior, and would continue bound till that same superior had reversed the sentence. Upon this a messenger was despatched to the desert after the holy anchorite, who ordered the grave to be opened and absolved the deceased, who, after this, continued in his grave in peace.

Pitton de Tournefort, in his *Voyage into the Levant*, gives the following interesting account : " We were present at a very different scene and one very barbarous at Myconi. The man, whose story we are going to relate, was a peasant of Myconi, naturally ill-natured and quarrelsome ; this is a circumstance to be taken notice of in such a case : he was murdered in the fields, nobody knew how or by whom. Two days after his being buried in a chapel in the town it was noised about that he was seen to walk about in the night with great haste, that he tumbled about other people's goods, put out their lamps, gripped them behind, and played a dozen other monkey tricks. At first the story was received with laughter, but the thing was looked upon seriously when the better sort of people began to complain of it : the papás themselves gave credit to the fact, and no doubt had their reasons for so doing ; masses were duly said ; but for all this the peasant drove his old trade and heeded nothing they could do. After divers meetings of the chief people of the city, of priests and monks, it was gravely concluded that it was necessary in consequence of some musty ceremonial to wait till the ninth day after the interment should be expired.

" On the tenth day they said one Mass in the chapel where the body was laid in order to drive out the demon which they imagined was got into it. After Mass they took up his body and got everything ready for blowing out his heart. . . . The corpse stunk so abominably that they were obliged to burn frankincense, but the smoke mixing with the exhalations from the carcase increased the stench ; every person averred that the blood of the corpse was extremely red. The butcher swore that the body was still warm. . . ."

Pitton concludes the story by ridiculing the theory that this was the body of a vampire or *vroucolaca.*

The practice of burning the body of a suspected or proved vampire does not appear to have found general favour in Greece, doubtless by reason of the fact that the Greeks possessed a religious horror of burning a body on which holy oil had been poured by the priest when performing the last rites upon the dying man.

Leake, whose *Travels in Northern Greece* were published in 1835, says in the fourth volume of that work : " It would be difficult now to meet with an example of the most barbarous of all these superstitions, the Vrukólaka. The name being Illyric, seems to acquit the Greeks of the invention, which was probably introduced into the country by the barbarians of Sclavonic race. Tournefort's description is admitted to be correct. The Devil is supposed to enter the Vrukólaka, who, rising from his grave, torments first his nearest relatives and then others, causing their death or loss of health. The remedy is to dig up the body and if, after it has been exorcised by the priest, the demon still persists in annoying the living, to cut it into small pieces, or, if that be not sufficient, to burn it."

In Crete the belief in vampires—or katalkanás, as the Cretans call them—and their existence and ill-deeds forms a general article of popular belief throughout the island, but is particularly strong in the mountains, and if anyone ventures to doubt it, undeniable facts are brought forward to silence the incredulous.

One of the stories told by the Cretans is as follows : " Once upon a time the village of Kalikráti, in the district of Sfakia, was haunted by a Katakhanás, and the people did not know what man he was or from what part he came. This Katakhanás destroyed both children and full-grown men, and desolated both that village and many others. They had buried him at the church of St George at Kalikráti, and in those times he was regarded as a man of note, and they had built an arch over his grave. Now a certain shepherd, believed to be his mutual Sýnteknos,[1] was tending his sheep and

---

[1] That is, related to each other through god-parents. In Crete, those whose god-parents were the same or were connected by ties of kinship were regarded as being in consanguineous relationship, and therefore were unable to contract marriages with each other.

goats near the church, and, on being caught
in a shower, he went to the sepulchre that he
might be protected from the rain. Afterwards he determined to sleep and pass the
night there, and, after taking off his arms, he
placed them by the stone which served him
as his pillow, crosswise. And people might
say that it was on this account that the
Katakhanás was not permitted to leave
his tomb. During the night, then, as he
wished to go out again, that he might
destroy men, he said to the shepherd:
'Gossip, get up hence, for I have some
business that requires me to come out.'
The shepherd answered him not, either the
first time, or the second, or the third;
further, he knew that the man had become
a Katakhanás, and that it was he who had
done all those evil deeds. On this account
he said to him on the fourth time of his
speaking: 'I shall not get up hence,
gossip, for I fear you are no better than you
should be and may do me some mischief;
but if I must get up, swear to me by your
winding-sheet that you will not hurt me,
and on that I will get up.' And he did not
pronounce the proposed words, but said
other things; nevertheless, when the shep-

herd did not suffer him to get up, he swore to
him as he wished. On this he got up, and,
taking his arms, removed them away from
the monument, and the Katakhanás came
forth, and, after greeting the shepherd, said
to him : ' Gossip, you must not go away, but
sit down here ; for I have some business
which I must go after ; but I shall return
within the hour, for I have something
to say to you.' So the shepherd waited
for him.

" And the Katakhanás went a distance of
about ten miles, where there was a couple recently married, and he destroyed them. On
his return the gossip saw that he was carrying some liver, his hands being moistened
with blood ; and, as he carried it, he blew
into it, just as the butcher does, to increase
the size of the liver. And he showed his
gossip that it was cooked, as if it had been
done on the fire. After this he said :
' Let us sit down, gossip, that we may
eat.' And the shepherd pretended to eat
it, but only swallowed dry bread, and kept
dropping the liver into his bosom. Therefore, when the hour for their separation
arrived, the Katakhanás said to the shepherd : ' Gossip, this which you have seen,

you must not mention, for if you do, my twenty nails will be fixed in your children and yourself.' Yet the shepherd lost no time, but gave information to the priests and others, and they went to the tomb, and there they found the Katakhanás, just as he had been buried. And all people became satisfied that it was he who had done all the evil deeds. On this account they collected a great deal of wood, and they cast him on it, and burnt him. His gossip was not present, but when the Katakhanás was already half-consumed, he, too, came forward in order that he might enjoy the ceremony. And the Katakhanás cast, as it were, a single spot of blood, and it fell on his foot, which wasted away, as if it had been roasted on a fire. On this account they sifted even the ashes, and found the little finger nail of the Katakhanás unburnt, and burnt it too."

The 22nd formula of the *Cuneiform Inscriptions of Western Asia*, published by Sir Henry Rawlinson and Mr Edwin Norris in 1866, reads :—

> The phantom, child of heaven,
> which the gods remember,
> the *Innin* (kind of hobgoblin) prince

of the lords
the . . . .
which produces painful fever,
the vampyre which attacks man,
the *Uruku* multifold
upon humanity,
may they never seize him !

CHAPTER IV

VAMPIRISM IN GREAT AND GREATER BRITAIN

WILLIAM OF NEWBURY, who flourished about the middle of the twelfth century, relates that in his time a man appeared corporeally in the county of Buckingham for three nights together, to his wife and, afterwards, to his other relatives. The way they took to defend themselves against his frightful visits was to stay up all night and make a noise when they observed that he was coming. Upon this he appeared to several people in broad day. Hereupon the Bishop of Lincoln summoned his council, and was informed that the thing was common in England, and that the only way to stop it which they knew of was to burn the spectre. The bishop did not relish this advice, as he thought the expedient a cruel one; but he wrote out a form of absolution on a scrap of paper and ordered it to be laid on the body of the deceased, which was found to be as fresh and entire as if it had been dead only a day ; and from that time the apparition was no more heard of. The author adds that these stories would be thought incredible if several instances of them had not happened in his time, attested by persons of undoubted credit.

The same author mentions a similar story, the *locale* of which was Berwick-on-Tweed, where the body was cut in pieces and burnt. Another vampire was burnt at Melrose Abbey. It was that of a very worldly priest who had been in his lifetime so fond of hunting that he was commonly called a *hundeprest*. A still more remarkable case occurred at a castle in the north of England, where the vampire so frightened all the people that no one ever ventured out of doors between sunset and sunrise. The sons of one of his supposed victims at length opened his grave and pierced his body, from which a great quantity of blood immediately flowed, which plainly proved that a large number of persons had been his victims.

4

Would Stoker have known this story?

At Waterford, in Ireland, there is a little graveyard under a ruined church near Strongbow's Tower. Legend has it that underneath the ground at this spot there lies a beautiful female vampire still ready to kill those she can lure thither by her beauty.

A vampire story is also related concerning an old Cumberland farmhouse, the victim being a girl whose screams were heard as she was bitten, and who only escaped with her life by thus screaming. In this case the monster was tracked to a vault in the churchyard, where forty or fifty coffins were found open, their contents mutilated and scattered around. One coffin only was untouched, and on the lid being taken off the form was recognised as being that of the apparition which had been seen, and the body was accordingly burnt, when the manifestations ceased.

In vol. iii. of *Borderland* Dr Franz Hartmann gave particulars of some vampire cases which had come under his observation.

" A young lady of G—— had an admirer, who asked her in marriage; but as he was a drunkard she refused and married another.

Thereupon the lover shot himself, and soon after that event a vampire, assuming his form, visited her frequently at night, especially when her husband was absent. She could not see him, but felt his presence in a way that could leave no room for doubt. The medical faculty did not know what to make of the case; they called it 'hysterics,' and tried in vain every remedy in the pharmacopœia, until she at last had the spirit exorcised by a man of strong faith."

Another case is that of a miller at D—— who had a healthy servant boy, who soon after entering his service began to fail in health. He had a ravenous appetite, but nevertheless grew daily more feeble. Being interrogated, he at last confessed that a thing which he could not see, but which he could plainly feel, came to him every night and sat upon his stomach, drawing all the life out of him, so that he became paralysed for the time being and could neither move nor cry out. Thereupon the miller agreed to share the bed with the boy, and proposed to him that he should give him a certain sign when the vampire arrived. This was done, and when the sign was given the miller grasped the invisible but very tangible substance that rested upon the boy's stomach, and although it struggled to escape, he grasped it firmly and threw it into the fire. After that the boy recovered his health and there was no repetition of the vampire's visits.

Dr Hartmann adds to this last account : " Those who, like myself, have on innumerable occasions removed astral tumours and thereby cured physical tumours will find the above not incredible nor inexplicable. Moreover, the above accounts do not refer to events of the past, but to persons still living in this country."

The following account is taken from the *Gentleman's Magazine* of July 1851 :—

"Singular Instance of Superstition,
A.D. 1629

" The Case, or, rather, History of a Case that happened in the County of Hereford in the fourth Year of the Reign of King Charles the First, which was taken from a MS. of Serjeant Mainard, who writes thus :

" ' I write the evidence which was given, which I and many others heard, and I write it exactly according to what was deposed

at the Trial at the Bar in the King's Bench.
Johan Norkot, the wife of Arthur Norkot,
being murdered, the question arose how she
came by her death. The coroner's inquest
on view of the body and deposition of Mary
Norkot, John Okeman and Agnes, his wife,
inclined to find Joan Norkot *felo de se*: for
they (*i.e.* the witnesses before mentioned)
informed the coroner and the jury that she
was found dead in the bed and her throat
cut, the knife sticking in the floor of the
room ; that the night before she was so
found she went to bed with her child (now
plaintiff in this appeal), her husband being
absent, and that no other person after such
time as she was gone to bed came into the
house, the examinants lying in the outer
room, and they must needs have seen if
any stranger had come in.   Whereupon the
jury gave up to the coroner their verdict
that she was *felo de se*.   But afterwards
upon rumour in the neighbourhood, and the
observation of divers circumstances that
manifested she did not, nor according to
these circumstances, possibly could, murder
herself, thereupon the jury, whose verdict
was not drawn into form by the coroner,
desired the coroner that the body which

was buried might be taken up out of the grave, which the coroner assented to, and thirty days after her death she was taken up, in the presence of the jury and a great number of the people, whereupon the jury changed their verdict. The persons being tried at Hertford Assizes were acquitted, but so much against the evidence that the judge (Harvy) let fall his opinion that it were better an appeal were brought than so foul a murder should escape unpunished.

" ' *Anno, paschœ termino, quarto Caroli,* they were tried on the appeal which was brought by the young child against his father, the grandfather and aunt, and her husband Okeman. And because the evidence was so strange I took exact and particular notes of it, which was as followeth, of the matters above mentioned and related, an ancient and grave person, the minister of the parish where the fact was committed, being sworn to give evidence according to custom, deposed, that the body being taken out of the grave thirty days after the party's death and lying on the grave and the four defendants present, they were required each of them to touch the dead body. O.'s wife fell on her knees and prayed God

to show token of their innocency, or to
some such purpose, but her very words I
forget.   The appellers did touch the dead
body, whereupon the brow of the dead,
which was all a livid or carrion colour (that
was the verbal expression in the terms of
the witness) began to have a dew or gentle
sweat, which reached down in drops on the
face, and the brow turned and changed to
a lively and fresh colour, and the dead
opened one of her eyes and shut it again,
and this opening the eye was done three
several times.   She likewise thrust out the
ring or marriage finger three times and
pulled it in again, and the finger dropt
blood from it on the grass.

" ' Hyde (Nicholas), Chief Justice, seem-
ing to doubt the evidence, asked the
witness :   " Who saw this beside yourself ? "

" ' Witness :   " I cannot swear that others
saw it ; but, my lord," said he, " I believe
the whole company saw it, and if it had
been thought a doubt, proof would have
been made of it, and many would have
attested with me."

" ' Then the witness observing some admiration in the auditors, he spoke further,

" My lord, I am minister of the parish, long
knew all the parties, but never had any
occasion of displeasure against any of
them, nor had to do with them, or they
with me, but as their minister. The thing
was wonderful to me, but I have no interest
in the matter, but am called upon to testify
the truth and that I have done."

" ' This witness was a reverend person
as I guess about seventy years of age.
His testimony was delivered gravely and
temperately, but to the good admiration
of the auditor. Whereupon, applying himself to the Lord Chief Justice, he said, " My
lord, my brother here present is minister
of the next parish adjacent, and I am
assured saw all done as I have affirmed,"
whereupon that person was also sworn to
give evidence, and he deposed the same in
every point, viz., the sweat of the brow,
the changes of its colour, the opening of
the eye, the thrice motion of the finger and
drawing it in again ; only the first witness
deposed that a man dipped his finger in the
blood to examine it, and swore he believed
it was real blood. I conferred afterwards
with Sir Edmund Vowel, barrister at law,
and others who concurred in this observa-

tion, and for myself, if I were upon my oath, can depose that these depositions, especially of the first witness, are truly here reported in substance.

" ' The other evidence was given against the prisoners, viz., against the grandmother of the plaintiff and against Okeman and his wife, that they lay in the next room to the dead person that night, and that none came into the house till they found her dead next morning, therefore if she did not murther herself, they must be the mur- therers, and to that end further proof was made.   First she lay in a composed manner in her bed, the bed cloaths nothing at all disturbed, and her child by her in the bed. Secondly, her throat was cut from ear to ear and her neck broken, and if she first cut her throat, she could not break her neck in the bed, nor *e contra*.   Thirdly, there was no blood in the bed, saving that there was a tincture of blood upon the bolster whereupon her head lay, but no other substance of blood at all.   Fourthly, from the bed's head on there was a stream of blood on the floor, till it ponded on the bending of the floor to a very great quan- tity and there was also another stream

of blood on the floor at the bed's feet,
which ponded also on the floor to another
great quantity but no other communica-
tion of blood on either of these places, the
one from the other, neither upon the bed,
so that she bled in two places severely, and
it was deposed that turning up the matte
of the bed, there were clotes of congealed
blood in the straw of the matte underneath.
Fifthly, the bloody knife in the morning
was found clinging in the floor a good distance from the bed, but the point of the
knife as it stuck in the floor was towards
the bed and the haft towards the door.
Sixthly, lastly, there was the brand of a
thumb and four fingers of a left hand on the
dead person's left hand.

" ' Hyde, Chief Justice : " How can you
know the print of a left hand from the print
of a right hand in such a case ? "

" ' Witness : " My lord, it is hard to
describe it, but if it please the honourable
judge (i.e. the judge sitting on the bench
beside the Chief Justice) to put his left
hand on your left hand, you cannot possibly place your right hand in the same
posture."

" ' It being done, and appearing so, the

defendants had time to make their defence,
but gave no evidence to that purpose.

" ' The jury departing from the bar and
returning, acquitted Okeman and found the
other three guilty ; who, being severally
demanded why judgment should not be
pronounced, sayd nothing, but each of
them said, " I did not do it." " I did not
do it." Judgment was made and the
grandmother and the husband executed,
but the aunt had the privilege to be spared
execution, being with child. I enquired
if they confessed anything at execution,
but did not as I was told.'

" Thus far the serjeant, afterwards Sir
John Mainard, a person of great note and
judgment in the law. The paper, of which
this is a copy, was found amongst his papers
since his death (1690) fair written with his
own hand. Mr Hunt of the Temple took
a copy of it, gave it me, which I have hereby
transcribed.—H.S."

It has been asserted by some writers that
the vampire is not to be found in Indian
lore and legend, and an attempt has been
made to connect this supposititious absence
of the blood-sucking demon with the Brah-
minical and Buddhistic vegetarian and

cremation customs. The Indian belief, however, in the existence of vampire spectres is as prevalent as it is in any other country, although the folk-lore and legends concerning them may, perhaps, be more scarce.

Fornari, in his *History of Sorcerers*, relates the following story : " In the beginning of the fifteenth century there lived at Bagdad an aged merchant who had grown wealthy in his business and who had an only son to whom he was tenderly attached. He resolved to marry him to the daughter of another merchant, a girl of considerable fortune, but without any personal attractions. Abul-Hassan, the merchant's son, on being shown the portrait of the lady, requested his father to delay the marriage till he could reconcile his mind to it. Instead, however, of doing this he fell in love with another girl, the daughter of a sage, and he gave his father no peace till he consented to the marriage with the object of his affections. The old man stood out as long as he could, but finding that his son was bent on acquiring the hand of the fair Nadilla, and was equally resolute not to accept the rich and ugly lady, he did what

most fathers under such circumstances
would do—he acquiesced.

" The wedding took place with great
pomp and ceremony, and a happy honey-
moon ensued, which might have been
happier but for one little circumstance
which led to very serious consequences.

" Abul-Hassan noticed that his bride
quitted the nuptial couch as soon as she
thought her husband was asleep, and did
not return to it till an hour before dawn.

" Filled with curiosity, Hassan one night,
feigning sleep, saw his wife rise and leave
the room. He rose, followed cautiously,
and saw her enter the cemetery. By the
straggling moonbeams he saw her go into
a tomb : he stepped in after her.

" The scene within was horrible. A
party of ghouls were assembled with the
spoils of the graves they had violated and
were feasting on the flesh of the long-
buried corpses. His own wife, who, by the
way, never touched supper at home, played
a no inconsiderable part in the hideous
banquet.

" As soon as he could safely escape
Abul-Hassan stole back to his bed.

" He said nothing to his bride till next

evening when supper was laid, and she
declined to eat; then he insisted on her
partaking, and when she positively refused
he exclaimed roughly : ' Oh yes, you keep
your appetite for your feasts with the
ghouls.' Nadilla was silent ; she turned
pale and trembled, and without a word
sought her bed. At midnight she rose, fell
on her husband with her nails and teeth,
tore his throat, and, having opened a vein,
attempted to suck his blood ; but Abul-
Hassan, springing to his feet, threw her
down and, with a blow, killed her. She
was buried next day.

"Three days after at midnight she reappeared, attacked her husband again, and
again attempted to suck his blood. He
fled from her and on the morrow opened
her tomb, burnt her to ashes and cast the
ashes into the Tigris."

There is a monstrous vampire which is
said to delight in sucking the blood of
children, and is known as a Pănangglan.
It has also a liking for sucking the blood
of women at childbirth ; but, as it is also
credited with a dread of thorns, the custom
has arisen of placing thorns about the rooms
of Indian houses on the occasions of births.

One of the Northern Indian witches—
the Jigar-Khor or Liver-eater—is believed
to be possessed of the power of being able
to steal the liver of another by looks and
incantations. A class of witches known as
Bhúts are said to have an extraordinary
fondness for fish, but also eat rice and all
kinds of human food.

Hugh Clifford, in his interesting work
In Court and Kampong, refers to the
" Pĕnangal, that horrible wraith of a woman
who has died in childbirth, and who comes
to torment small children in the guise of a
fearful face and bust with many feet of
bloody, trailing entrails in her wake,"
also of that " weird little white animal, the
Mati-ânak, that makes beast noises round
the graves of children ; and of the familiar
spirits that men raise up from the corpses
of babes who have never seen the light, the
tips of whose tongues they bite off and
swallow, after the child has been brought
back to life by magic agencies."

In the Tamil dream of Harichándra, the
frenzied Sandramáti says to the king :
" I belong to the race of elves, for I killed
thy child in order that I might feed on its
delicate flesh." The Vetala is said to feed

chiefly on corpses. The Bhúts and other dismal ravenous ghosts, who are dreaded at the moon-wane of the month Katik (October–November), were not supposed to devour men, but only their food.

Then there is the Hántu Sàburo, which chases men into the forest by means of his dogs, and if they are run down he drinks their blood. The Hántu Dondong resides in caves and crevices in rocks. He kills dogs and wild hogs with the sumpitan, and then drinks their blood. The Hántu Parl fastens on to the wound of an injured person and sucks the blood.

Barth, in his *History of Religions* (Hinduism), says that " Siva is identified with *Mrityu*, Death, and his old name *Pacupati*, Lord of herds, acquires the ominous meaning of Master of human cattle. He is chief of the mischievous spirits, of ghouls and vampires that frequent places of execution and those where the dead are buried, and he prowls about with them at nightfall."

Other classes of demons are also known as the *Rakshasas* or the *Pisâchâs*, a word which literally means " flesh-eaters," which Delongchamps has translated as " bloodthirsty savages," but other etymologists actually as " vampires."

The vampire demon is no stranger to Australia. Bonwick, in his *Daily Life of the Tasmanians*, tells us that : " During the whole of the first night after the death of one of their tribe they will sit round the body, using rapidly a low, continuous recitative to prevent the evil spirit from taking it away. This evil spirit was the ghost of an enemy. Fires at night kept off these mischievous beings, which were like the vampires of Europe."

CHAPTER V

VAMPIRISM IN GERMANY AND SURROUNDING COUNTRIES

GERMANY, the home of modern philosophy, is not free from the belief in the reality of the vampire apparition, although the more horrible forms of the superstition are not frequently encountered. Crosses are, however, frequently erected at the head, or by the side, of graves, even in Protestant cemeteries, in order that their presence may prevent the occupants from being controlled by any demon that might, but for the presence of such charm, take possession of a body; and the *Nachzehrer* is as much dreaded in many parts of Germany as the *Vrykolaka* is in Russia. In some parts of the Kaiser's dominions, food is still buried with the corpse in order to assuage any pangs of hunger that may arise; and even when this is not done, a few grains

Nachzehrer — literally means afterwards (Nach) devourer (zehrer) — prominent in Silesia, Bavaria, + Kashubes of Northern Europe

GERMANY AND OTHER COUNTRIES 67

of corn or rice are scattered upon the grave as a survival of the ancient custom. In Diesdorf it is believed that if money is not placed in the mouth of a dead person at burial, or his name not cut from his shirt, he will, in all probability, become a Nachzehrer, and his ghost issue from the grave in the form of a pig. Another sure preventive of such a calamity is to break the neck of a dead body.

The following story was contributed by Dr Franz Hartmann to the *Occult Review* for September 1909, under the title of "An Authenticated Vampire Story":—

"On June 10th, 1909, there appeared in a prominent Vienna paper (the *Neues Wiener Journal*) a notice saying that the castle of B—— had been burned by the populace, because there was a great mortality among the peasant children, and it was generally believed that this was due to the invasion of a vampire, supposed to be the last Count B——, who died and acquired that reputation. The castle was situated in a wild and desolate part of the Carpathian Mountains, and was formerly a fortification against the Turks. It was not inhabited, owing to its being believed to be in the possession of ghosts; only a wing of it was used as a dwelling for the caretaker and his wife.

" Now it so happened that, when I read the above notice, I was sitting in a coffee-house at Vienna in company with an old friend of mine who is an experienced occultist and editor of a well-known journal, and who had spent several months in the neighbourhood of the castle. From him I obtained the following account, and it appears that the vampire in question was probably not the old Count, but his beautiful daughter, the Countess Elga, whose photograph, taken from the original painting, I obtained. My friend said : ' Two years ago I was living at Hermannstadt, and being engaged in engineering a road through the hills, I often came within the vicinity of the old castle, where I made the acquaintance of the old castellan, or caretaker, and his wife, who occupied a part of the wing of the house, almost separate from the main body of the building. They were a quiet old couple and rather reticent in giving information or expressing an opinion in regard to the strange noises which were often heard at night in the deserted halls, or of the apparitions which the Wallachian peasants claimed to have seen when they loitered in the surroundings after dark. All I could gather was that the old Count was a widower and had a beautiful daughter, who was one day killed by a fall from her horse, and that soon after the old man died in some mysterious manner, and the bodies were buried in a solitary graveyard belonging to a neighbouring village. Not long after their death an unusual mortality was noticed among the inhabitants of the village : several children and even some grown people died without any apparent illness ; they merely wasted away ; and thus a rumour was started that the old Count had become a vampire after his death. There is no doubt that he was not a saint, as he was addicted to drinking, and some shocking tales were in circulation about his conduct and that of his daughter ; but whether there was any truth in them, I am not in a position to say.

" ' Afterwards the property came into the possession of ——, a distant relative of the family, who is a young man and officer in a cavalry regiment at Vienna. It appears that the heir enjoyed his life at the capital

and did not trouble himself much about
the old castle in the wilderness ; he did not
even come to look at it, but gave his
directions by letter to the janitor, telling
him merely to keep things in order and to
attend to repairs, if any were necessary.
Thus the castellan was actually master of
the house, and offered its hospitality to me
and my friends.

"One evening I and my two assistants, Dr E——, a young lawyer, and
Mr W——, a literary man, went to inspect
the premises. First we went to the stables.
There were no horses, as they had been
sold ; but what attracted our special attention was an old, queer-fashioned coach
with gilded ornaments and bearing the
emblems of the family. We then inspected
the rooms, passing through some halls and
gloomy corridors, such as may be found
in any old castle. There was nothing
remarkable about the furniture ; but in
one of the halls there hung in a frame an
oil-painting, a portrait, representing a lady
with a large hat and wearing a fur coat. We
were all involuntarily startled on beholding
this picture—not so much on account of
the beauty of the lady, but on account of

the uncanny expression of her eyes; and Dr E——, after looking at the picture for a short time, suddenly exclaimed: 'How strange! The picture closes its eyes and opens them again, and now it begins to smile!'

"Now Dr E—— is a very sensitive person, and has more than once had some experience in spiritism, and we made up our minds to form a circle for the purpose of investigating this phenomenon. Accordingly, on the same evening we sat around a table in an adjoining room, forming a magnetic chain with our hands. Soon the table began to move and the name *Elga* was spelled. We asked who this Elga was, and the answer was rapped out: 'The lady whose picture you have seen.'

"'Is the lady living?' asked Mr W——. This question was not answered; but instead it was rapped out: 'If W—— desires it, I will appear to him bodily to-night at two o'clock.' W—— consented, and now the table seemed to be endowed with life and manifested a great affection for W——; it rose on two legs and pressed against his breast, as if it intended to embrace him.

" We inquired of the castellan whom the
picture represented ; but to our surprise
he did not know. He said that it was the
copy of a picture painted by the celebrated
painter Hans Markart of Vienna, and had
been bought by the old Count because its
demoniacal look pleased him so much.

" We left the castle, and W—— retired
to his room at an inn a half-hour's journey
distant from that place. He was of a
somewhat sceptical turn of mind, being
neither a firm believer in ghosts and apparitions nor ready to deny their possibility. He was not afraid, but anxious to
see what would come of his agreement,
and for the purpose of keeping himself
awake he sat down and began to write an
article for a journal.

" Towards two o'clock he heard steps on
the stairs and the door of the hall opened ;
there was the rustling of a silk dress and the
sound of the feet of a lady walking to and
fro in the corridor.

" It may be imagined that he was somewhat startled ; but taking courage, he said
to himself : ' If this is Elga, let her come in.'
Then the door of the room opened and
Elga entered. She was most elegantly

dressed, and appeared still more youthful and seductive than the picture. There was a lounge on the other side of the table where W—— was writing, and there she silently posted herself. She did not speak, but her looks and gestures left no doubt in regard to her desires and intentions.

" Mr W—— resisted the temptation and remained firm. It is not known whether he did so out of principle or timidity or fear. Be this as it may, he kept on writing, looking from time to time at his visitor and silently wishing that she would leave. At last, after half an hour, which seemed to him much longer, the lady departed in the same manner in which she came.

" This adventure left W—— no peace, and we consequently arranged several sittings at the old castle, where a variety of uncanny phenomena took place. Thus, for instance, once the servant-girl was about to light a fire in the stove, when the door of the apartment opened and Elga stood there. The girl, frightened out of her wits, rushed from the room, tumbling down the stairs in terror with the lamp in her hand, which broke, and came very near to setting her clothes on fire. Lighted lamps and candles went out when brought near the picture, and many other ' manifestations ' took place which it would be tedious to describe; but the following incident ought not to be omitted.

"Mr W—— was at that time desirous of obtaining the position as co-editor of a certain journal, and a few days after the above-narrated adventure he received a letter in which a noble lady of high position offered him her patronage for that purpose. The writer requested him to come to a certain place the same evening, where he would meet a gentleman who would give him further particulars. He went, and was met by an unknown stranger, who told him that he was requested by the Countess Elga to invite Mr W—— to a carriage drive, and that she would await him at midnight at a certain crossing of two roads, not far from the village. The stranger then suddenly disappeared.

"Now it seems that Mr W—— had some misgivings about the meeting and drive, and he hired a policeman as detective to go at midnight to the appointed place, to see what would happen. The policeman went and reported next morning that he had seen nothing but the well-known, old-fashioned carriage from the castle, with two black horses, standing there as if waiting for somebody, and that as he had no occasion to interfere, he merely waited until the carriage moved on. When the castellan of the castle was asked, he swore that the carriage had not been out that night, and in fact it could not have been out, as there were no horses to draw it.

" But that is not all, for on the following day I met a friend who is a great sceptic and disbeliever in ghosts, and always used to laugh at such things. Now, however, he seemed to be very serious and said : ' Last night something very strange happened to me. At about one o'clock this morning I returned from a late visit, and as I happened to pass the graveyard of the village, I saw a carriage with gilded ornaments standing at the entrance. I wondered about this taking place at such an unusual hour, and being curious to see what would happen, I waited. Two elegantly dressed ladies issued from the carriage. One of these was young and pretty, but threw at me a devilish and scornful look as they both passed by and entered

the cemetery. There they were met by a
well-dressed man, who saluted the ladies
and spoke to the younger one, saying :
" Why, Miss Elga ! Are you returned so
soon ? " Such a queer feeling came over
me that I abruptly left and hurried home.'

" This matter has not been explained ;
but certain experiments which we subse-
quently made with the picture of Elga
brought out some curious facts.

" To look at the picture for a certain
time caused me to feel a very disagreeable
sensation in the region of the solar plexus.
I began to dislike the portrait and proposed
to destroy it. We held a sitting in the
adjoining room ; the table manifested a
great aversion to my presence. It
was rapped out that I should leave the
circle, and that the picture must not be
destroyed. I ordered a Bible to be brought
in, and read the beginning of the first
chapter of St John, whereupon the above-
mentioned Mr E—— (the medium) and
another man present claimed that they saw
the picture distorting its face. I turned
the frame and pricked the back of the
picture with my penknife in different places,
and Mr E——, as well as the other man,

Why a pentagram + Not a cross?, Or some other symbol?.

felt all the pricks, although they had retired to the corridor.

" I made the sign of the pentagram over the picture, and again the two gentlemen claimed that the picture was horribly distorting its face.

" Soon afterwards we were called away and left that country. Of Elga I heard nothing more."

Thus far goes the account of my friend the editor.

Siegbert's *Chronicle* for the year 858 has the following story : " There appeared this year in the diocese of Mentz a spirit which discovered himself at first by throwing stones and beating against the walls of houses, as if it had been with a great mallet. He then proceeded to speak and reveal secrets, and discovered the authors of several thefts and other matters likely to breed disturbances in the neighbourhood. At last he vented his malice upon one particular person, whom he was industrious in persecuting and making odious to all the neighbours by representing him as the cause of God's anger against the whole village. The spirit never forsook the poor man, but tormented him without inter-

mission, burnt all his corn in the barns,
and set every place on fire where he came.
The priests attempted to frighten him away
by exorcisms, prayers, and holy water;
but the spectre answered them with a
volley of stones which wounded several of
them.   When the priests were gone he was
heard to bemoan himself and say that he
was forced to take refuge in the cowl of
one of the priests, who had injured the
daughter of a man of consequence in the
village.   He continued in this manner to
infest the village for three years together,
and never gave over till he had set every
house in it on fire."

CHAPTER VI

VAMPIRISM IN HUNGARY, BAVARIA, AND SILESIA

THE Hungarians believe that those who have been passive vampires in life become active vampires after death; that those whose blood has been sucked in life by vampires become themselves vampires after death. In many districts the belief also prevails that the only way to prevent this calamity happening is for the threatened victim to eat some earth from the grave of the attacking vampire, and to smear his own body with blood from the body of that vampire.

That the belief in vampirism is still current in Hungary was evidenced recently. The *Daily Telegraph* of February 15th, 1912, contained the following paragraph: " A Buda-Pesth telegram to the *Messaggero* reports a terrible instance of superstition.

79

Eating grave dirt — can this be related to Dracula carrying dirt with him — connection to the particular grave?

A boy of fourteen died some days ago in a small village. A farmer, in whose employment the boy had been, thought that the ghost of the latter appeared to him every night. In order to put a stop to these supposed visitations, the farmer, accompanied by some friends, went to the cemetery one night, stuffed three pieces of garlic and three stones in the mouth, and thrust a stake through the corpse, fixing it to the ground. This was to deliver themselves from the evil spirit, as the credulous farmer and his friends stated when they were arrested."

In 1732, in a village in Hungary, in the space of three months, seventeen persons of different ages died of vampirism, some without being ill, and others after languishing two or three days. It is reported that a girl named Stanoska, daughter of the Heyduk Jotiutso, who went to bed in perfect health, awoke in the middle of the night trembling violently and uttering terrible shrieks, declaring that the son of the Heyduk Millo, who had been dead nine weeks, had nearly strangled her in her sleep. She fell into a languid state and died at the end of three days. Young Millo was exhumed and found to be a vampire.

Calmet, in his work *The Phantom World*, relates the following : " About fifteen years ago a soldier who was billeted at the house of a Haidamaque peasant, on the frontiers of Hungary, as he was one day sitting at table near his host, the master of the house, saw a person he did not know come in and sit down to table also with them. The master of the house was strangely frightened at this, as were the rest of the company. The soldier knew not what to think of it, being ignorant of the matter in question. But the master of the house being dead the very next day, the soldier inquired what it meant. They told him it was the body of the father of the host, who had been dead and buried for ten years, who had thus come to sit down next to him, and had announced and caused his death.

" The soldier informed the regiment of it in the first place, and the regiment gave notice of it to the general officers, who commissioned the Count de Cabreras, captain of the regiment of Alandetti infantry, to make information concerning this circumstance. Having gone to the place with some other officers, a surgeon and an auditor, they heard the depositions of all

6

the people belonging to the house, who decided unanimously that the ghost was the father of the master of the house, and that all the soldier had said and reported was the exact truth, which was confirmed by all the inhabitants of the village.

"In consequence of this the corpse of the spectre was exhumed and found to be like that of a man who had just expired, and his blood like that of a living man. The Count de Cabreras had his head cut off and caused him to be laid again in the tomb. He also took information concerning other similar ghosts : among others, of a man dead more than thirty years who had come back three times to his house at meal-time. The first time he had sucked the blood from the neck of his own brother, the second time from one of his sons, and the third time from one of the servants in the house ; and all three died of it instantly and on the spot. Upon this deposition the commissary had this man taken out of his grave, and finding that, like the first, his blood was in a fluidic state like that of a living person, he ordered them to run a large nail into his temple and then to lay him again in the grave.

Why did the victims die instantly?

" He caused a third to be burned who
had been buried more than sixteen years
and had sucked the blood and caused the
death of two of his sons. The commissary
having made his report to the general
officers, was deputed to the Emperor,
who commanded that some officers both
of war and of justice, some physicians and
surgeons and some learned men should be
sent to examine the causes of these extraordinary events. The person who related
these particulars to us had heard them
from the Count de Cabreras at Fribourg in
1730."

Raufft tells the story of a man named
"Peter Plogojowitz, an inhabitant of a
village in Hungary called Kisolova, who,
after he had been buried more than ten
years, appeared by night to several persons
in the village, while they were asleep, and
squeezed their throats in such a manner
that they expired within twenty-four hours.
There died in this way no less than nine
persons in eight days ; and the widow of
this Plogojowitz deposed that she herself
had been visited by him since his death, and
that his errand was to demand his shoes ;
which frightened her so much that she at

once left Kisolova and went to live somewhere else.

"These circumstances determined the inhabitants of the village to dig up the body
of Plogojowitz and burn it, in order to put
a stop to such troublesome visits. Accordingly they applied to the commanding
officer of the Emperor's troops in the
district of Gradisca, in the kingdom of
Hungary, and to the incumbent of the place,
for leave to dig up the corpse. They both
made a great many scruples about granting
it ; but the peasants declared plainly that if
they were not permitted to dig up this accursed carcase, which they were fully con-
vinced was a vampire, they would be forced
to leave the village and settle where they
could.

"The officer who gave this account, seeing
that there was no hindering them either
by fair means or foul, came in person,
accompanied by the minister of Gradisca,
to Kisolova, and they were both present
at the digging up of the corpse, which they
found to be free from any bad smell, and
perfectly sound, as if it had been alive,
except that the tip of the nose was a little
dry and withered. The beard and hair were

grown fresh and a new set of nails had sprung up in the room of the old ones that had fallen off. Under the former skin, which looked pale and dead, there appeared a new one, of a natural fresh colour ; and the hands and feet were as entire as if they belonged to a person in perfect health. They observed also that the mouth of the vampire was full of fresh blood, which the people were persuaded had been sucked by him from the persons he had killed.

"The officer and the divine having diligently examined into all the circumstances, the people, being fired with fresh indignation, and growing more fully persuaded that this carcase was the real cause of the death of their countrymen, ran immediately to fetch a sharp stake, which being driven into his breast, there issued from the wound, and also from his nose and mouth, a great quantity of fresh, ruddy blood ; and something which indicated a sort of life, was observed to come from him. The peasants then laid the body upon a pile of wood, and burnt it to ashes."

Calmet says he was told by M. de Vassimont, who was sent to Moravia by Leopold, first Duke of Lorraine, that he was in-

formed by public report that it was common
enough in that country to see men who had
died some time before present themselves
in a party and sit down to the table with
persons of their acquaintance without saying
anything, but that nodding to one of the
party he would infallibly die some days
afterwards.   M. de Vassimont received con-
firmation of this story from several persons,
amongst others an old curé who said he
had seen more than one instance of it.
The priest added that the inhabitants had
been delivered from these troublesome
spectres owing to the fact that their corpses
had been taken up and burned or destroyed
in some way or other.

At the beginning of the eighteenth century
several vampire investigations were held
at the instigation of the Bishop of Olmutz.
The village of Liebava was particularly
infested, and a Hungarian placed himself
on the top of the church tower and just
before midnight saw a well-known vampire
issue from his tomb, and, leaving his
winding-sheet behind him, proceed on his
rounds.   The Hungarian descended from
the tower and took away the sheet and
ascended the tower again.   When the vam-

pire returned he flew into a great fury
because of the absence of the sheet. The
Hungarian called to him to come up to the
tower and fetch it. The vampire mounted
the ladder, but just before he reached the
top the Hungarian gave him a blow on the
head which threw him down to the churchyard. His assailant then descended, cut
off the vampire's head with a hatchet, and
from that time the vampire was no more
heard of.

In 1672 there dwelt in the market town
of Kring, in the Archduchy of Krain, a man
named George Grando, who died, and was
buried by Father George, a monk of St
Paul, who, on returning to the widow's
house, saw Grando sitting behind the door.
The monk and the neighbours fled. Soon
stories began to circulate of a dark figure
being seen to go about the streets by night,
stopping now and then to tap at the door
of a house, but never to wait for an answer.
In a little while people began to die mysteri-
ously in Kring, and it was noticed that the
deaths occurred in the houses at which the
spectred figure had tapped its signal. The
widow Grando also complained that she
was tormented by the spirit of her husband,

who night after night threw her into a deep sleep with the object of sucking her blood. The Supan, or chief magistrate, of Kring decided to take the usual steps to ascertain whether Grando was a vampire. He called together some of the neighbours, fortified them with a plentiful supply of spirituous liquor, and they sallied off with torches and a crucifix.

Grando's grave was opened, and the body was found to be perfectly sound and not decomposed, the mouth being opened with a pleasant smile, and there was a rosy flush on the cheeks. The whole party were seized with terror and hurried back to Kring, with the exception of the Supan. The second visit was made in company with a priest, and the party also took a heavy stick of hawthorn sharpened to a point. The grave and body were found to be exactly as they had been left. The priest kneeled down solemnly and held the crucifix aloft: "O vampire, look at this," he said; "here is Jesus Christ who loosed us from the pains of hell and died for us upon the tree!"

He went on to address the corpse, when it was seen that great tears were rolling down the vampire's cheeks. A hawthorn stake was brought forward, and as often as they strove to drive it through the body the sharpened wood rebounded, and it was not until one of the number sprang into the grave and cut off the vampire's head that the evil spirit departed with a loud shriek and a contortion of the limbs.

Similar stories to this were continually being circulated from the borders of Hungary to the Baltic.

At one time the spectre of a village herdsman near Kodom, in Bavaria, began to appear to several inhabitants of the place, and either in consequence of their fright or from some other cause, every person who had seen the apparition died during the week afterwards. Driven to despair, the peasants disinterred the corpse and pinned it to the ground with a long stake. The same night he appeared again, plunging people into convulsions of fright, and suffocated several of them. Then the village authorities handed the body over to the executioner, who caused it to be carried into a field adjoining the cemetery, where it was burned. The corpse howled like a madman, kicking and tearing as if it had been alive.

When it was run through again with sharp-pointed stakes, before the burning, it uttered piercing cries and vomited masses of crimson blood. The apparition of the spectre ceased only after the corpse had been reduced to ashes.

Fortis, in his *Travels into Dalmatia*, says that the Moslacks have no doubt as to the existence of vampires, and attribute to them, as in Transylvania, the sucking of the blood of infants. Therefore, when a man dies, and he is suspected of vampirism, or of being a *vukodlak*—the term they employ—they cut his hams and prick his whole body with pins, pretending that he will be unable to walk about after this operation has been performed. There are even instances of Moolacchi who, imagining that they may possibly thirst for human blood after death, particularly the blood of children, entreat their heirs, and sometimes even make them promise, to treat them in this manner directly after death.

Dr Henry More, in his *Antidote against Atheism*, argues for the reality of vampires, and relates the following stories.

"A shoemaker of Breslau, in Silesia, in

1591 terminated his life by cutting his throat. His family, however, spread abroad the report that he had died of apoplexy, which enabled them to bury him in the ordinary way and save the disgrace of his being interred as a suicide. Despite this, however, the rumour got abroad that the man had committed suicide. It was also reported that his ghost had been seen at the bedsides of several persons, and the rumours and reports spreading, it was decided by the authorities to disinter the body. It had been buried on September 22nd, 1591, and the grave was opened on April 18th, 1592. The body was found to be entire; it was not in any way putrid, the joints were flexible, there was no ill smell, the wound in the throat was visible and there was no corruption in it. There was also observed what was claimed to be a magical mark on the great toe of the right foot— an excrescence in the form of a rose. The body was kept above ground for six days, during which time the apparitions still appeared. It was then buried beneath the gallows, but the apparition still came to the bedsides of the alarmed inhabitants, pinching and suffocating people, and leaving marks of its fingers plainly visible on the flesh. A fortnight afterwards the body was again dug up, when it was observed to have sensibly increased its size since its last interment. Then the head, arms, and legs of the corpse were cut off; the heart, which was as fresh and entire as that in a freshly killed calf, was also taken out of the body. The whole body thus dismembered was consigned to the flames and the ashes thrown into the river. The apparition was never seen afterwards. A servant of the deceased man was also said to have acted in a similar manner after her death. Her remains were also dug up and burned, and then her apparition ceased to torment the inhabitants.''

"Johannes Cuntius, a citizen and alderman of Pentach, in Silesia, when about sixty years of age, died somewhat suddenly, as the result of a kick from his horse. At the moment of his death a black cat rushed into the room, jumped on to the bed, and scratched violently at his face. Both at the time of his death and that of his funeral a great tempest arose — the wind and snow ' made men's bodies quake and their

teeth chatter in their heads.' The storm
is said to have ceased with startling sudden-
ness as the body was placed under the ground.
Immediately after the burial, however,
stories began to circulate of the appearance of a phantom which spoke to people
in the voice of Cuntius. Remarkable tales
were told of the consumption of milk from
jugs and bowls, of milk being turned into
blood, of old men being strangled, children
taken out of cradles, altar-cloths being
soiled with blood, and poultry killed and
eaten. Eventually it was decided to disinter the body. It was found that all the
bodies buried above that of Cuntius had
become putrefied and rotten, but his skin
was tender and florid, his joints by no
means stiff, and when a staff was put
between his fingers they closed around it
and held it fast in their grasp. He could
open and shut his eyes, and when a vein
in his leg was punctured the blood sprang
out as fresh as that of a living person.
This happened after the body had been in
the grave for about six months. Great
difficulty was experienced when the body
was cut up and dismembered, by the order
of the authorities, by reason of the resist-

ance offered ; but when the task was completed, and the remains consigned to the flames, the spectre ceased to molest the natives or interfere with their slumbers or health."

CHAPTER VII

VAMPIRISM IN SERVIA AND BULGARIA

THE document which gives the particulars of the following remarkable story is signed by three regimental surgeons and formally countersigned by the lieutenant-colonel and sub-lieutenant, and bears the date June 7th, 1732, with the address Meduegna, near Belgrade.

" In the spring of 1727 there returned from the Levant to the village of Meduegna, near Belgrade, one Arnod Paole, who, in a few years' military service and varied adventure, had amassed enough to purchase a cottage and an acre or two of land in his native place, where he gave out that he meant to pass the remainder of his days. He kept his word. Arnod had yet scarcely reached the prime of manhood ; and though he must have encountered the rough as well as the smooth of life, and have mingled with many a wild and reckless companion, yet his natural good disposition and honest principles had preserved him unscathed in the scenes he had passed through. At all events, such were the thoughts expressed by his neighbours as they discussed his return and settlement among them in the stube of the village hof. Nor did the frank and open countenance of Arnod, his obliging habits and steady conduct, argue their judgments incorrect. Nevertheless, there was something occasionally notice-able in his ways, a look and tone that be-trayed inward disquiet. He would often refuse to join his friends, or on some sudden plea abruptly quit their society. And he still more unaccountably, and it seemed systematically, avoided meeting his pretty neighbour, Nina, whose father occupied the next farm to his own. At the age of seventeen Nina was as charming a picture of youth, cheerfulness, innocence, and con-fidence as you could have seen in all the world. You could not look into her limpid eye, which steadily returned your gaze, with-out seeing to the bottom of the pure and transparent spring of her thoughts. Why then did Arnod shrink from meeting her ?

He was young; had a little property; had
health and industry; and he had told his
friends he had formed no ties in other
lands. Why then did he avoid the fascina-
tion of the pretty Nina, who seemed a being
made to chase from any brow the clouds
of gathering care? But he did so, yet
less and less resolutely, for he felt the
charm of her presence. Who could have
done otherwise? And how long he resisted the impulse of his fondness for
the innocent girl who sought to cheer his
fits of depression!

"And they were to be united—were betrothed; yet still the anxious gloom would
fitfully overcast his countenance, even in
the sunshine of those hours.

"'What is it, dear Arnod, that makes
you sad? It cannot be on my account, I
know, for you were sad before you noticed
me; and that, I think surely, first made
me notice you.'

"'Nina,' he answered, 'I have done, I
fear, a great wrong in trying to gain your
affections. Nina, I have a fixed impression
that I shall not live; yet, knowing this, I
have selfishly made my existence necessary
to your happiness.'

7

" ' How strangely you talk, dear Arnod! Who in the village is stronger and healthier than you ? You feared no danger when you were a soldier. What danger do you fear as a villager of Meduegna ? '

" ' It haunts me, Nina.'

" ' But, Arnod, you were sad before you thought of me. Did you then fear to die ? '

" ' Oh, Nina, it is something worse than death.' And his vigorous frame shook with agony.

" ' Arnod, I conjure you, tell me.'

" ' It was in Cossova this fate befell me. Here you have hitherto escaped the terrible scourge. But there they die, and the dead visit the living. I experienced the first frightful visitation, and I fled ; but not till I had sought his grave and executed the dread expiation from the vampire.'

" Nina's blood ran cold. She stood horror-stricken. But her young heart soon mastered her first despair. With a touching voice she spoke: 'Fear not, dear Arnod; fear not now. I will be your shield, or I will die with you ! '

" And she encircled his neck with her gentle arms, and returning hope shone, Iris-

like, amid her falling tears. Afterwards they
found a reasonable ground for banishing
or allaying their apprehension in the lengthy
time which had elapsed since Arnod left
Cossova, during which no fearful visitant
had again approached him; and they
fondly protested *that* gave them security.

"One day about a week after this conversation Arnod missed his footing when
on the top of a loaded hay-waggon, and
fell from it to the ground. He was picked
up insensible, and carried home, where,
after lingering a short time, he died. His
interment, as usual, followed immediately.
His fate was sad and premature. But
what pencil could paint Nina's grief?

"Twenty or thirty days after his decease,
several in the neighbourhood complained
that they were haunted by the deceased
Arnod; and what was more to the purpose,
four of them died. The evil looked at
sceptically was bad enough, but aggravated
by the suggestions of superstition it spread
a panic through the whole district. To
allay the popular terror, and, if possible,
to get at the root of the evil, a determina-
tion was come to publicly to disinter the
body of Arnod, with the view of ascertain-

ing whether he really was a vampire, and, in that event, of treating him conformably. The day fixed for these proceedings was the fortieth after his burial.

"It was on a grey morning in early August that the commission visited the cemetery of Meduegna, which, surrounded with a wall of stone, lies sheltered by the mountain that, rising in undulating green slopes, irregularly planted with fruit-trees, ends in an abrupt craggy ridge, covered with underwood. The graves were, for the most part, neatly kept, with borders of box, or something like it, and flowers between, and at the head of most, a small wooden cross, painted black, bearing the name of the tenant. Here and there a stone had been raised. One of terrible height, a single narrow slab, ornamented with grotesque Gothic carvings, dominated over the rest. Near this lay the grave of Arnod Paole, towards which the party moved. The work of throwing out the earth was begun by the grey, careful old sexton, who lived in the Leichenhaus beyond the great crucifix. Near the grave stood two military surgeons or *feldscherers* from Belgrade, and a drummer-boy, who held their case of instruments. The boy looked on with keen interest; and when the coffin was exposed and rather roughly drawn out of the grave, his pale face and bright, intent eye showed how the scene moved him. The sexton lifted the lid of the coffin; the body had become inclined to one side. Then, turning it straight: 'Ha, ha! What? Your mouth not wiped since last night's work?'

"The spectators shuddered; the drummer-boy sank forward, fainting, and upset the instrument case, scattering its contents; the senior surgeon, infected with the horror of the scene, repressed a hasty exclamation. They threw water on the drummer-boy and he recovered, but would not leave the spot. Then they inspected the body of Arnod. It looked as if it had not been dead a day. After handling it, the scarfskin came off, but below were *new skin and new nails*! How could they have come there but from this foul feeding? The case was clear enough: there lay before them the thing they dreaded—the vampire! So, without more ado, they simply drove a stake through poor Arnod's chest, whereupon a quantity

of blood gushed forth, and the corpse
uttered a dreadful groan.

" ' Murder !   Murder ! '   shrieked   the
drummer-boy, as he rushed wildly, with
convulsed gestures, from the scene."

The body of Arnod was then burnt to
ashes, which were returned to the grave.
The authorities further staked and burnt
the bodies of the four others who were
supposed to have been infected by Arnod.
No mention is made of the state in which
they were found.   The adoption of these
decisive measures failed, however, entirely
to extinguish the evil, which continued
still to hang about the village.   About five
years afterwards it had again become very
rife, and many died through it ; whereupon
the authorities determined to make another
and a complete clearance of the vampire
in the cemetery, and with that object
they had all the graves, to which suspicion attached, opened, and their contents
officially anatomised, and the following are
abridgments of the medical reports :—

1. A woman of the name of Stana,
twenty years of age, who had died three
months before, of a three days' illness
following her confinement.   She had before

her death avowed that she had *anointed* herself with the blood of a vampire, to liberate herself from his persecution. Nevertheless she had died. Her body was entirely free from decomposition. On opening it the chest was found filled with recently effused blood, and the bowels had exactly the appearance of sound health. The skin and nails of her hands and feet were loose and came off, but underneath were new skin and nails.

2. A woman of the name of Miliza, who had died at the end of a three months' illness. The body had been buried ninety and odd days. In the chest was liquid blood. The viscera were as in the former instance. The body was declared by a heyduk, who recognised it, to be in better condition and fatter than it had been in the woman's legitimate lifetime.

3. The body of a child eight years old, that had likewise been buried ninety days; it was in the vampire condition.

4. The son of a heyduk, named Milloc, sixteen years old. The body had lain in the grave nine weeks. He had died after three days' indisposition, and was in the condition of a vampire.

5. Joachim, likewise the son of a heyduk, seventeen years old. He had died after three days' illness ; had been buried eight weeks and some days ; was found in the vampire state.

6. A man of the name of Rusha, who had died of an illness of ten days' duration and had been six weeks buried, in whom likewise fresh blood was found in the chest.

7. The body of a girl ten years of age who had died two months before. It was likewise in the vampire state, perfectly undecomposed, with blood in the chest.

8. The body of the wife of one Hadnuck, buried seven weeks before ; and that of her infant eight weeks old, buried only twenty-one days. They were both in a state of decomposition, though buried in the same ground and closely adjoining the others.

9. A servant, by name Rhade, twenty-three years of age ; he had died after an illness of three months' duration, and the body had been buried five weeks. It was in a state of decomposition.

10. The body of the heyduk Stanco, sixty years of age, who had died six weeks previously. There was much blood and

other fluid in the chest and abdomen, and the body was in a vampire condition.

11. Millac, a heyduk, twenty-five years old. The body had been in the earth six weeks. It was also in the vampire condition.

12. Stanjoika, the wife of a heyduk, twenty years old; had died after an illness of three days, and had been buried eighteen. The countenance was florid. There was blood in the chest and in the heart. The viscera were perfectly sound, the skin remarkably flush.

The vampire tradition in its original loathsomeness, however, is to be found only in the Bulgarian provinces, whither the knowledge of the superstition was first imported from Dalmatia and Albania. In the former country the vampire is known by the name of *wukodlak*.

St Clair and Brophy, in their work on Bulgaria, state that in Bulgaria the vampire is no longer a dead body possessed by a demon, but a soul in revolt against the inevitable principle of corporeal death. He is detected by a hole in the tombstone which is placed over his grave, which hole is filled up by the medicine man with dirt mixed with poisonous herbs.

Vampirism is claimed to be hereditary as well as epidemic and endemic, and vampires are also stated to be capable of exercising considerable physical force. Stories are told of men who have had their jaws broken, as well as their limbs, as the result of their struggles with vampires.

About 1863 there was a local epidemic of vampirism in one of the villages of Bulgaria, when the place became so infested by them that the inhabitants were forced to assemble together in two or three houses, burn candles at night, and watch by turns in order to avoid the assaults made by the Obours, who lit up the streets with their sparkles. Some of the most enterprising of these threw their shadows on the walls of the rooms where the peasants were assembled through fear, while others howled and shrieked and swore outside the door, entered the abandoned houses, spat blood on the floors, turned everything topsy-turvy, and smeared everything, even the pictures of the saints, with cow-dung, until an old lady, suspected of witchcraft, discovered and laid the troublesome spirit, and afterwards the village was free.

When the Bulgarian vampire has finished his forty days' apprenticeship to the world of shadows, he rises from the tomb in bodily form, and is able to pass himself off as a human being living in the natural manner.

In Slavonic countries the vampire is said to be possessed of only one nostril, but is credited with possessing a sharp point at the end of his tongue, like the sting of a bee.

In Bulgaria one method of abolishing the vampire is said to be by bottling him. The sorcerer, armed with the picture of some saint, lies in ambush until he sees the vampire pass, when he pursues him with his picture. The vampire takes refuge in a tree or on the roof of a house, but his persecutor follows him up with the talisman, driving him away from all shelter in the direction of a bottle specially prepared, in which is placed some favourite food of the vampire. Having no other alternative, he enters this prison, and is immediately fastened down with a cork on the interior of which is a fragment of an eikon or holy picture. The bottle is then thrown into the fire and the vampire disappears for ever.

In Bulgaria the vampire does not invariably seem to have the thirst for human blood, unless there happens to be a shortage in his human food—a distinction which marks him from the species found in other countries.

CHAPTER VIII

THE Slavonic belief in vampires is one of the characteristic features of their creed.

The Little Russians hold that, if the vampire's hands have grown numb from remaining long crossed in the grave, he makes use of his teeth, which are like steel. When he has gnawed his way with these through all obstacles, he first destroys the babies he finds in a house, and afterwards the older inmates. If fine salt be scattered on the floor of a room, the vampire's footsteps may be traced to his grave, in which he will be found resting with rosy cheek and gory mouth.

The Kashoubes say that when a *vieszcy*, as they call a vampire, wakes from his sleep within the grave he begins to gnaw his hands and feet, and as he gnaws, first his relatives, and then his neighbours, sicken

Is this Russian folk belief a physical or spiritual (or both) belief?

and die. When he has finished his own store of flesh, he rises at midnight and destroys cattle or climbs a belfry and sounds the bell. All who hear the ill-omened tones will soon die. Generally he sucks the blood of sleepers.

Ralston, in his *Songs of the Russian People,* says that it is in the Ukraine and in White Russia—so far as the Russian Empire is concerned—that traditions are most rife about this ghastly creation of morbid fancy, and that the Little Russians attribute the birth of a vampire to an unholy union between a witch and a werwolf or a devil.

He relates the following as a specimen of the vampire stories prevalent in the country :—

"A peasant was driving past a graveyard after it had grown dark. After him came running a stranger, dressed in a red shirt and a new jacket, who said : 'Stop ! Take me as your companion.'

"' Pray take a seat.'

"They enter a village, drive up to this and that house. Though the gates are wide open, yet the stranger says, 'Shut tight !' for on those gates crosses have been branded. They drive on to the very last house : the gates are barred, and from them hangs a padlock weighing a score of pounds; but there is no cross there, and the gates open of their own accord.

"They go into the house: there on the bench lie two sleepers—an old man and a lad. The stranger takes a pail, places it near the youth, and strikes him on the back; immediately the back opens, and forth flows rosy blood. The stranger fills the pail full and drinks it dry. Then he fills another pail with blood from the old man, slakes his brutal thirst, and says to the peasant: 'It begins to grow light! Let us go back to my dwelling.'

"In a twinkling they find themselves at the graveyard. The vampire would have clasped the peasant in his arms, but luckily for him the cocks begin to crow, and the corpse disappears. The next morning, when folks come and look, the old man and the lad are dead."

According to the Servians and Bulgarians, unclean spirits enter into the corpses of malefactors and other evilly disposed persons, who then become vampires. In some places the jumping of a boy over the corpse is considered as fatal as that of a cat.

There is a story told of a mother who lived

in Saratof who cursed her son, and his body remained free from corruption after burial for a hundred years. When it was disinterred, his aged mother, who is said to have been still alive, pronounced his pardon, and, at that very moment, the corpse crumbled into dust.

The Russians say that, when driving a stake into the body of a vampire, this must be done by one single blow, as a second blow will reanimate the corpse.

One group of Russian stories relate to the sudden resuscitation shortly after death of wizards and witches at midnight possessed with the longing to eat the flesh of the watchers around the bier. The stories go that the body of the suspected witch was generally enclosed in a coffin which was secured with iron bands and carried to the church, and a watcher was appointed to read aloud from the Scriptures over the coffin right through each night until burial. It was also the duty of the watcher to draw on the floor a magic circle, within which he must stand and hold in his hand a hammer, the ancient weapon of the thunder-god. If the suspicion that the individual was a wizard or witch was a correct one, a mighty wind would arise one night about twelve o'clock, the iron bands of the coffin would give way with a terrible crash, the coffin-lid fall off, and the corpse leap forth and, uttering a terrible screech, rush at the watcher, who, if he had not taken the prescribed precautions, would fall a victim to the monster, and in the morning there would be nothing left of him but his bare bones. The following story of this character is contained in the records of the Kharkof government:—

"Once, in the days of old, there died a terrible sinner. His body was taken into the church, and the sacristan was told to read some psalms over him. He took the precaution to catch a cock and carry it with him to the church. At midnight the dead man leaped from his coffin, opened wide his jaws, and rushed at his victim; but, at that moment, the sacristan gave the bird a hard pinch. The cock uttered his usual crow, and at the same moment the dead man fell backwards to the ground a numb, motionless corpse."

The following story is also given by Ralston in his collection of Russian folk-stories:—

8

The Coffin Lid

" A moujik was driving along one night
with a load of pots. His horse grew tired,
and all of a sudden it came to a standstill
alongside of a graveyard. The moujik un-
harnessed his horse and set it free to graze ;
meanwhile he laid himself down on one of
the graves. But somehow he didn't go to
sleep.

" He remained there some time. Suddenly
the grave began to open beneath him ; he
felt the movement and sprang to his feet.
The grave having opened, out of it came a
corpse, wrapped in a white shroud, and
holding a coffin lid. He ran to the church,
laid the coffin lid at the door, and then set
off for the village.

" The moujik was a daring fellow. He
picked up the coffin lid and remained
standing beside his cart, waiting to see what
would happen. After a short delay the
dead man came back, and was going to
snatch up his coffin lid—but it was not to
be seen. Then the corpse began to track
it out, traced it up to the moujik, and said :
' Give me my lid ; if you don't, I'll tear
you to bits ! '

"'And my hatchet—how about that?' answered the moujik. 'Why, it's I who'll be chopping you into small pieces!'

"'Do give it back to me, good man!' begs the corpse.

"'I'll give it when you tell me where you've been and what you've done.'

"'Well, I've been in the village, and there I've killed a couple of youngsters.'

"'Well, then, tell me how they can be brought back to life.'

"The corpse reluctantly made answer: 'Cut off the left skirt of my shroud. Take it with you, and when you come into the house where the youngsters were killed, pour some live coals into a pot and put the piece of the shroud in with them, and then lock the door. The lads will be revived by the smoke immediately.'

"The moujik cut off the left skirt of the shroud and gave up the coffin lid. The corpse went to its grave—the grave opened. But just as the dead man was descending into it, all of a sudden the cocks began to crow, and he had not time to get properly covered over. One end of the coffin lid remained standing out of the ground.

"The moujik saw all this and made a note

of it. The day began to dawn ; he harnessed his horse and drove into the village.
In one of the houses he heard cries and
wailing. In he went—there lay two dead
lads.

" ' Don't cry,' said he ; ' I can bring them
to life.'

" ' Do bring them to life, kinsman,' said
their relatives. ' We'll give you half of all
we possess.'

" The moujik did everything as the corpse
had instructed him, and the lads came back
to life. Their relatives were delighted, but
they immediately seized the moujik and
bound him with cords, saying : ' No, no,
trickster ! We'll hand you over to the
authorities. Since you know how to bring
them back to life, maybe it was you who
killed them ! '

" ' What are you thinking about, true
believers ? Have the fear of God before
your eyes ! ' cried the moujik.

" Then he told them everything that had
happened to him during the night. Well,
they spread the news through the village,
and the whole population assembled and
stormed into the graveyard. They found
the grave from which the dead man had

come out; they tore it open, and they
drove an aspen stake right into the heart
of the corpse, so that it might no more rise
up and slay. But they rewarded the
moujik handsomely, and sent him home
with great honour.'

The Soldier and the Vampire

" A certain soldier was allowed to go home
on furlough. Well, he walked and walked
and walked, and after a time he began to
draw near to his native village. Not far off
from that village lived a miller in his mill.
In old times, the soldier had been very
intimate with him : why shouldn't he go
and see his friend ? He went. The miller
received him cordially, and at once brought
out liquor ; and the two began drinking
and chattering about their ways and doings.
All this took place towards nightfall, and
the soldier stopped so long at the miller's
that it grew quite dark.

When he proposed to start for his village,
his host exclaimed : ' Spend the night
here, trooper ; it is very late now, and
perhaps you may run into mischief.'

" ' How so ? '

" ' God is punishing us ! A terrible warlock has died among us, and by night he rises from his grave, wanders through the village, and does such things as bring fear upon the very bailiffs; and so how could you help being afraid of him?'

"'Not a bit of it! A soldier is a man who belongs to the Crown, and Crown property cannot be drowned in water or burned in fire. I will be off. I am tremendously anxious to see my people as soon as possible.'

"Off he set. His road lay in front of a graveyard. On one of the graves he saw a great fire blazing. What is that? Then he said: 'Let's have a look.' When he drew near, he saw that the warlock was sitting at the fire, sewing boots.

"'Hail, brother!' calls out the soldier.

"The warlock looked up and said: 'What have you come here for?'

"'Why, I wanted to see what you were doing.'

"The warlock threw his work aside and invited the soldier to a wedding.

"'Come along, brother,' says he; 'let's enjoy ourselves. There is a wedding going on in the village.'

"'Come along,' says the soldier.

"They came to where the wedding was; they were given drink, and treated with the utmost hospitality. The warlock drank and drank, revelled and revelled, and then grew angry. He chased all the guests and relatives out of the house, threw the wedded pair into a slumber, took out two phials and an awl, pierced the hands of the bride and bridegroom with the awl, and began drawing off their blood. Having done this, he said to the soldier: 'Now, let's be off.'

"Accordingly, they went off. On the way the soldier said: 'Tell me, why did you draw off their blood in those phials?'

"'Why, in order that the bride and bridegroom might die. To-morrow morning no one will be able to wake them. I alone know how to bring them back to life.'

"'How's that managed?'

"'The bride and bridegroom must have cuts made in their heels, and some of their blood must then be poured back into these wounds. I've got the bridegroom's blood stowed away in my right-hand pocket, and the bride's in my left.'

"The soldier listened to this without letting a single word escape him. Then the warlock began boasting again.

" ' Whatever I wish,' says he, ' that I can do.'

" ' I suppose it's quite impossible to get the better of you,' says the soldier.

" ' Impossible ?   If anyone were to make a pyre of aspen boughs, a hundred loads of them, and were to burn me on that pyre, then he'd be able to get the better of me. Only he'd have to look sharp in burning me, for snakes and worms and different kinds of reptiles would creep out of my inside, and crows and magpies and jackdaws would come flying up.   All these must be caught and flung on the pyre.   If so much as a single maggot were to escape, then there'd be no help for it.   In that maggot I should slip away.'

" The soldier listened to all this and did not forget it.   He and the warlock talked and talked, and at last they arrived at the grave.

" ' Well, brother,' said the warlock, ' now I'll tear you to pieces, otherwise you'll be telling all this.'

" ' What are you talking about ?   Don't you deceive yourself, for I serve God and the Empire.'

" The warlock gnashed his teeth, howled

aloud, and sprang at the soldier, who drew his sword and began laying about him with sweeping blows. They struggled and struggled; the soldier was all but at the end of his strength. 'Ah,' thinks he, 'I'm a lost man, and all for nothing!' Suddenly the cocks began to crow. The warlock fell lifeless to the ground.

" The soldier took the phials of blood out of the warlock's pockets, and went to the house of his own people. When he had got there and exchanged greetings with his relatives, they said: 'Did you see any disturbance, soldier?'

" 'No, I saw none.'

" 'There, now! Why, we've a terrible piece of work going on in the village. A warlock has taken to haunting it.'

" After talking a while they lay down to sleep. The next morning the soldier awoke and began asking: 'I'm told you've got a wedding going on somewhere here.'

" 'There was a wedding in the house of a rich moujik,' replied his relatives, 'but the bridegroom has died this very night— what from nobody knows.'

" 'Where does this moujik live?'

" They showed him the house. Thither

he went without speaking a word. When he got there he found the whole family in tears.

"'What are you mourning about?' says he.

"'Such and such is the state of things, soldier,' say they.

"'I can bring your young people to life again. What will you give me if I do?'

"'Take what you like, even were it half of what we have got.'

"The soldier did as the warlock had instructed him, and brought the young people back to life. Instead of weeping there began to be happiness and rejoicing: the soldier was hospitably treated and well rewarded. Then—left about face! Off he marched to Starosta and told the burgomaster to call the peasants together and to get ready a hundred loads of aspen wood. Well, they took the wood into the graveyard, dragged the warlock out of his grave, placed him on the pyre, and set it in flames. The warlock began to burn. His corpse burst, and out of it came snakes, worms, and all kinds of reptiles, and up came flying crows, magpies, and jackdaws. The peasants knocked them down and flung them into the fire, not allowing so much as a single maggot to creep away! And so the warlock was thoroughly consumed, and the soldier collected his ashes and strewed them to the winds. From that time there was peace in the village.

" The soldier received the thanks of the whole community."

In Russian folk-lore there is a class of demons known as " heart devourers," who touch their victim with an aspen or other twig credited with magical properties ; the heart then falls out and may be replaced by some baser one. There is a Moscovian story in which a hero awakes with the heart of a hare, the work of a demon while the man was asleep. He remained a coward for the rest of his life. In another instance a very quiet, reserved, inoffensive peasant received a cock's heart in exchange for his own, and afterwards was for ever crowing like a healthy bird.

The following is taken from the *Lettres Juives* of 1738 :—

" In the beginning of September there died in the village of Kisilova, three leagues from Graditz, an old man who was sixty-two years of age. Three days

after he had been buried, he appeared
in the night to his son, and asked him
for something to eat; the son having given
him something, he ate and disappeared.
The next day the son recounted to his
neighbours what had happened. That
night the father did not appear, but the
following night he showed himself and asked
for something to eat. They know not
whether the son gave him anything or not;
but the next day he was found dead in his
bed. On the same day, five or six persons
fell suddenly ill in the village, and died one
after the other in a few days.

" The officer or bailiff of the place, when
informed of what had happened, sent an
account of it to the tribunal of Belgrade,
which despatched to the village two of
these officers and an executioner to examine
into this affair. The imperial officer from
whom we have this account repaired thither
from Graditz to be a witness of what took
place.

" They opened the graves of those who had
been dead six weeks. When they came to
that of the old man, they found him with
his eyes open, having a fine colour, with
natural respiration, nevertheless motion-

less as the dead : whence they concluded
that he was most undoubtedly a vampire.
The executioner drove a stake into his
heart ; they then raised a pile and reduced
the corpse to ashes.   No mark of vampirism
was found either on the corpse of the son or
on the others."

The following story is told by Madame
Blavatsky in *Isis Unveiled,* who states that
she had the account from an eye-witness
of the occurrence :—

"About the beginning of the nineteenth
century there occurred in Russia one of the
most frightful cases of vampirism on record.
The governor of the province of Tch——
was a man of about sixty years of age, of a
cruel and jealous disposition.   Clothed with
despotic authority, he exercised it without
stint, as his brutal instincts prompted.   He
fell in love with the pretty daughter of a
subordinate officer.   Although the girl was
betrothed to a young man whom she loved,
the tyrant forced her father to consent to
his having her marry him ; and the poor
victim, despite her despair, became his
wife.   His jealous disposition soon exhibited
itself.   He beat her, confined her to her
room for weeks together, and prevented her

seeing anyone except in his presence. He finally fell sick and died. Finding his end approaching, he made her swear never to marry again, and with fearful oaths threatened that in case she did he would return from his grave and kill her. He was buried in the cemetery across the river, and the young widow experienced no further annoyance until, getting the better of her fears, she listened to the importunities of her former lover, and they were again betrothed.

" On the night of the customary betrothal feast, when all had retired, the old mansion was aroused by shrieks proceeding from her room. The doors were burst open, and the unhappy woman was found lying on her bed in a swoon. At the same time a carriage was heard rumbling out of the courtyard. Her body was found to be black and blue in places, as from the effect of pinches, and from a slight puncture in her neck drops of blood were oozing. Upon recovering, she stated that her deceased husband had suddenly entered her room, appearing exactly as in life, with the exception of a dreadful pallor ; that he had upbraided her for her inconstancy, and then beaten and pinched her most cruelly. Her story was disbelieved; but the next morning the guard stationed at the other end of the bridge which spans the river reported that just before midnight a black coach-and-six had driven furiously past without answering their challenge.

"The new governor, who disbelieved the story of the apparition, took nevertheless the precaution of doubling the guards across the bridge. The same thing happened, however, night after night, the soldiers declaring that the toll-bar at their station near the bridge would rise of itself, and the spectral equipage would sweep past them, despite their efforts to stop it. At the same time every night the watchers, including the widow's family and the servants, would be thrown into a heavy sleep; and every morning the young victim would be found bruised, bleeding, and swooning as before. The town was thrown into consternation. The physicians had no explanations to offer; priests came to pass the night in prayer, but as midnight approached, all would be seized with the same terrible lethargy. Finally the archbishop of the province came and performed

the ceremony of exorcism in person. On
the following morning the governor's widow
was found worse than ever. She was now
brought to death's door.

"The governor was finally driven to take
the severest measures to stop the ever-
increasing panic in the town. He stationed
fifty Cossacks along the bridge, with orders
to stop the spectral carriage at all hazards.
Promptly at the usual hour it was heard
and seen approaching from the direction
of the cemetery. The officer of the guard
and a priest bearing a crucifix planted
themselves in front of the toll-bar and
together shouted: 'In the name of God
and the Czar, who goes there?' Out of
the coach was thrust a well-remembered
head, and a familiar voice responded:
'The Privy Councillor of State and Governor C—— !' At the same moment the
officer, the priest, and the soldiers were
flung aside, as by an electric shock, and
the ghostly equipage passed them before
they could recover breath.

"The archbishop then resolved as a last
expedient to resort to the time-honoured
plan of exhuming the body and driving an
oaken stake through its heart. This was

done with great religious ceremony in the presence of the whole populace. The story is that the body was found gorged with blood, and with red cheeks and lips. At the instant that the first blow was struck upon the stake a groan issued from the corpse and a jet of blood spouted high into the air. The archbishop pronounced the usual exorcism, the body was reinterred, and from that time no more was heard of the vampire."

CHAPTER IX

THE belief in vampires, ghouls, and lamies, all of which are more or less similar, appears to have been known from time immemorial among the Arabs and Persians. The *Thousand and One Nights* and many other Oriental stories turn on this subject, and the terrible superstition is still believed in by the Arabs. Plato and Democritus say (and traces of this belief are not unknown among the Semites), that souls lived for a certain time close to their dead bodies, which they sometimes preserved from corruption, and that they could cause the hair, beard, and nails to grow in their tombs. The early Christians also believed that the dead could come out of their sepulchres to make room for more exalted personages, when these

were interred close to them. St John the
Almoner died at Amathonte in the Isle of
Cyprus, and his body was placed between
the bodies of two bishops who had passed
away some years previously. They immediately withdrew on either side to make
room for the saint. When Heloise died she
asked to be buried in the same tomb as her
lover, Abelard, who, although he had pre-
deceased her by more than twenty years,
extended his arms at her approach and
received her into his care.

In a suburb of Bagdad there was living
at the commencement of the fifteenth
century an elderly merchant who had
amassed a considerable fortune, and who
had no one to inherit all his wealth save a
son whom he loved tenderly. He decided
to give him as wife the daughter of one of
his friends, a merchant like himself, with
whom he had become on intimate terms
during his many voyages. This young
woman was very rich, but at the same time
very plain, and the son, Abdul-Hassan,
when he was shown her portrait, asked for
time that he might consider the matter.

One evening, when he was taking a
solitary ramble in the clear light of the

moon in the country round about Bagdad,
he heard a melodious voice singing some
verselets from the Qur-án to the accompani-
ment of a guitar. He crossed rapidly to
the grove in which the singer was hidden,
and found himself at the foot of a rustic
house, where he saw, on a balcony covered
with climbing creepers, a woman more
fascinating than the houris. He dared to
approach her only by signs of respect and
love, and, her window being closed, he
returned home without knowing whether
she had seen him.

The following morning, after the first
prayer, that said on the rising of the sun, he
went to the place where he had seen this
charming girl, for whom he felt already an un-
quenchable love. He made many inquiries,
and ascertained, not without some trouble,
that his charmer was seventeen years of
age, unmarried, and that she was the
daughter of a wise man who had no dowry
to bestow upon her, but that she was well
instructed in all the noble sciences : which
information served to increase the young
man's admiration.

From that moment the marriage project
of his father became impossible. The young

man went to him and said, "Father, you know that up till now I have never failed to obey you: to-day I ask you to allow me to choose my own wife." He then told his father of the repugnance he felt towards the young woman selected for him, and of his love for the charming unknown.

The father raised several objections, but seeing that his son was led by a fatalism that was irresistible, he placed no more obstacles in the way of his happiness; he went to the abode of the wise man and asked for the hand of his daughter for his son. The two lovers met, saw and adored, and the marriage was made.

At the end of three months, passed in rapture and pleasure, Abdul-Hassan, awakening in the middle of the night, perceived that his young wife had left the bed-chamber. At first he took no heed and resolved to await her return, but grew anxious when this was delayed until exactly an hour before daylight. He noticed that his wife, whose name was Nadilla, came into the room with a frightened look and a mysterious manner; but her husband feigned sleep and determined to take no notice then of the mystery, though he was firmly resolved to arrive at its solution as quickly as possible.

Nadilla said nothing to her husband regarding her absence during the night, and on their retirement into the bed-chamber the following night, after kissing her husband and bidding him good-night, she quietly loosened herself from his embrace, and leaving him, as she thought, in a sound slumber, went out, evidently according to her custom. Abdul-Hassan hastily dressed himself and followed her from a a distance, but making many detours. Finally he saw her enter the cemetery, into which he also followed. He saw his wife lower herself into a large tomb which was lighted by three funerary lamps. Great was his horror when he looked into the tomb and found his young and beautiful wife, seated among several ghouls, partaking of a barbarous feast. He then remembered that since his marriage his wife had always abstained from food during the evening, but this fact had not made more than a passing impression.

Presently he saw one of the ghouls bring in a newly buried corpse, around which the company ranged themselves.

For a moment the thought came to him to reveal himself and so disperse the hideous sorcerers, but he had not sufficient courage. The corpse was cut into pieces and eaten by the ghouls, who meantime chanted their infernal songs. At the end of the horrid feast they interred the bones, and separated after mutual embraces.

Abdul-Hassan, who had no desire to be seen, hastened to regain his bed, on which he threw himself and feigned sleep until the morning. He made no sign throughout the day that he had been the witness of anything untoward on the previous night. But when evening came and he pressed his wife to join him at the meal, Nadilla excused herself, according to her custom. He began to insist, but still she refused, until, losing his temper, he called out : " You prefer to go to supper with the ghouls."

Nadilla made no reply, but, pale and trembling with fury, she went in silence to bed alongside her husband. In the middle of the night, when she thought her husband was plunged in a deep sleep, she said to him in a low, angry tone : " Now then, expiate your sacrilegious curiosity." At the same time she put her knee on his chest, seized

him by the throat, opened a vein, and began
to drink his blood. All this was the work
of an instant.

The young husband was not asleep, and
escaping quickly from the arms of the fury,
struck her a blow with a poignard and left
her dying by the side of the couch. Immediately he called for help to dress the
wound she had made, and on the following
day the remains of the ghoul-wife were duly
interred.

Three   nights   afterwards   the   wife
appeared, threw herself upon her husband,
and tried to strangle him. The poignard
of Abdul-Hassan was useless, and his only
safety lay in a speedy flight.

On the following day he caused Nadilla's
tomb to be opened, and found the body, to
all appearances, to be full of life and
seemingly breathing while in her coffin. He
went to the house of the man who had
passed himself off as her father, and heard
from him a remarkable story. He said
that his daughter had been married two
years previously to one of the Caliph's
officers, but, having delivered herself up
to the most infamous debaucheries, had
been killed by her husband. She had,

however, come to life again in the tomb, and had then returned to her father's house.

The body was then exhumed, burned on a pyre of scented wood, the cinders thrown into the Tigris, and thus Arabia was delivered of a monster.

Of course the story is pure fiction, but it will serve to convey an idea of the beliefs of the Arabs. In the *Contes Orientaux* of Caylus there is the story of a vampire who was only able to preserve his life by devouring from time to time the heart of a young man.

The ancients gave to the souls of the wicked and to those who died a violent death the name of Lemures. These Lemures were believed to become real vampires, and we learn from Apuleius, Ovid, and other ancient authors that these spectres only appeared in order to menace, frighten, and torment the living. The Romans so dreaded these apparitions that they instituted religious ceremonies for the purpose of appeasing them, which ceremonies they called by the name of Lemuria. Dion Chrysostom tells us that the Lemures, or Lamies, as he terms them, were numerous in Lybia. Among Orientals the Lamies were supposed to dig up the dead bodies in

the cemeteries and hold great festivals on
their flesh.

In Isaiah xxxiv. 14 there is a prophecy
of the ruin of Babylon, foretelling that it
would become (according to the marginal
readings) the abode of lamies and strygie.
Now *strygia* is merely another name for
vampire.   There is in Salic Law an ordin-
ance against these monsters : " If a strygia
has eaten a man, and has been convicted of
the crime, he will pay a fine of eight
thousand deniers, equal to two hundred
golden sous." Strygie were common in
the fifth century, and another article in the
same law inflicts a penalty of 187 sous and
a half on anyone who called a free woman
a strygia or a prostitute.   As these strygie
were liable to fines and penalties, some
have thought that the name was applied
exclusively to magicians ; but, in those
times, spectres and phantoms, as well as
human beings and animals, were the subject
of laws.   The *Capitularies* of Charlemagne
and of Louis the Debonnair, imposed fines
and penalties on fiery phantoms which
appeared in the air, although those luminous
apparitions appeared to be nought else
than the aurora borealis.   Charlemagne con-

demned to death those who had executed
men or women accused of being strygie.
The text makes use of the words *stryga vel
masca,* and scholars assert that this last
term, like *larva,* means a spectre or
phantom. From cap. vi of the Capitularies
it will be seen that it was a general belief
among the Saxons that there were sorcerers
and spectres who sucked the blood and ate
the flesh of living beings, that they were burnt
when discovered, and that the people, in order
to protect themselves from these monsters
in turn, ate the flesh of these strygie.

A feature of some vampires is not the
eating of human flesh and drinking of
blood, but satisfaction of the passions by
carnal connection with a living person
through the medium of a dead body, sometimes its own corpse. One such remarkable instance, even to the very date of its
occurrence, is related by several French
authors. On the 1st of January 1613 a
young Parisian gentleman was returning
home about four o'clock in the afternoon,
after having spent the earlier part of the
day in company with some friends. In
a short passage, or porch, which led into
his house, he saw a young woman, appar-

ently wealthy, seeking protection there
from the heavy rain, which was then
descending. She was wearing a richly
embroidered silk gown, enriched with a
string of valuable pearls, and wearing also
several other beautiful jewels and gems,
all apparently genuine. She apologised
for the intrusion, but craved permission to
remain there until the return of her servant,
whom she had despatched for her carriage.
The gentleman willingly gave his consent,
but entreated her to enter the dwelling,
and, after many protestations, she consented. The time passed but neither the
servant nor the carriage put in an appearance. When the time for the evening
meal arrived her host placed before her
the best that his larder contained, and they
enjoyed the meal together. As the storm
had not abated, he persuaded her to remain
for the night, offering her accommodation
in a separate room from his own. She
consented, but later, after they had both
retired and the servants also had been
dismissed for the night, the host went to
his guest's room on the plea of inquiring
if she was comfortable. He held her
hand, and mutual kisses were, after a

while, exchanged. Then, yielding to his entreaties, she gave him permission to join her, which he did, and shortly afterwards went back to his own chamber.

In the morning he sent his servant to inquire if the guest needed anything, and the servant returned with a message that the lady did not wish to arise then, as she had had but little sleep during the night. The host went out for a walk, and on his return went up himself to his guest's room. He drew aside the curtain and spoke to her in endearing terms, but, receiving no reply, clutched her by the arm, which, to his horror, he found to be as cold as ice, and the body, on examination, proved to be lifeless. A magistrate and some doctors were summoned, and on their arrival they were unanimous in the opinion that the body was that of a young woman that had been hanged some time previously, and ventured the opinion that a spectre or devil or, perhaps, the young woman herself, had inhabited it for the time being for the gratification of unlawful desires. This had scarcely been said when there arose from the bed a big, thick cloud of smoke, which lasted for a few seconds only, then gradually vanished, when it was found that the dead body had also disappeared.

William of Paris relates that a soldier, having slept with a beautiful girl, found, on the following morning, a stinking carcass by his side.

St Hippolytus often saw a beautiful woman, who loved him, and who presented herself naked before him, pressed herself against him, and forced her caresses upon him. The saint, becoming wearied of these importunities, says the legend, threw his stole around her neck and strangled her. Afterwards he found frequently in his arms an evil-smelling corpse which he recognised as the body of a woman who had been dead for many years.

A citizen of Lyons was compelled to sleep for three years with the ghost of his wife, whom he had assassinated. The spectre would allow him no rest, but with its hideous and bloody form tormented and punished him continually. Madame de Genlis made this story the basis of her romance, *Chevaliers du Cygne*.

Although, perhaps, somewhat remote, there appears to be a connection between the vampire belief and the funerary feasts

of olden times, and even of modern times
in some countries, Ireland not excepted.
It was regarded as a very solemn duty
among idolatrous people to offer sumptuous
repasts to the gods of the infernal regions.
The superstition, always believed, when
once introduced, quickly inspired people
to offer to the ghosts of the departed the
same honours which they had previously
offered to the infernal gods.

The magnificence of those feasts, the
profound silence observed during their
celebrations, the darkness in which they
took place, the sight of the tombs with the
skulls and bones of the departed, their
partly corrupted bodies, just dimly seen
by the pale light of the funerary torches,
the prostration and consternation of the
guests, who held the arms of the corpses
while inviting them to take part in the
feast—what more likely to inspire horror ?
Yet it was regarded as one of the most
sacred religious duties to solemnise those
nocturnal festivals. In Egypt, where the
utmost respect has always been evinced
for the departed, where tombs have never
inspired aught but veneration, these nocturnal feasts always followed immediately

after the solemnity of interment. In
Rome funerals were always followed by
a silent feast, which the heir gave to his
relatives and to the friends who reposed
near by. Formerly in Courland and in
Middle Gaul, immediately a citizen had
drawn his last breath, he was arrayed in
his best clothes, a sum of money was
placed in his hands, or by his side, as well
as some food. The body was then placed
in the coffin and taken to the grave, which
was always a long distance from the town
and generally in a field or a forest. The
mourners ate and drank on the journey,
but it was regarded as a serious offence not
to salute the departed always when eating
and drinking, and to invite the corpse to
partake of the nourishment with the living.

In earlier times it was the custom to
offer the deceased only honey, eggs, milk,
bread, and wine, but when manners became
more ferocious, the people yielded to the
belief that the souls of the departed found
greater pleasure in drinking blood than in
partaking of the fruits of the earth. This
foolish and cruel idea caused them first
of all to sprinkle on tombs the blood of
animals, and, afterwards, human blood.

Wives, concubines, slaves, captives who had belonged to the departed, whose memory they wished to honour, offered themselves to the knives of the priests. It was in the midst of those horrible sacrifices, amid the noise of the wailings of the victims, that the funerary feasts were partaken. Then, excited by wine and the horror of the spectacle, they called upon the deceased, and believing they saw his soul under the guise of a hideous spectre, a horrible phantom, they called out: " Ghost, you have risen from your tomb ; is it to come with us, to eat and to drink with us ? "

When this barbarous festival was ended, and they believed the ghost to be satisfied ; when there were no more unfortunate victims to immolate, and when, perhaps, the guests felt the torments of remorse, they implored the ghost—which their heated imagination caused them to address as though he were really present—to withdraw, but, above all, to do no injury to his friends.

These same cruelties and ceremonies were at one time religiously observed by the savages of America. In some parts of Louisiana, immediately a woman of noble

10

birth, that is to say, one of the race of the sun, died, it was the custom to strangle on her tomb a dozen children and fourteen adults, who were buried with her; and this same superstition which led to the immolation of these victims, changed them into ghosts, which the people believed they could see at night wandering around the tomb, and afterwards appearing in the immediate neighbourhood as vampires.

In thus giving food and blood to the departed the people thought this recognition of their wants would accord protection to those who thus honoured them; while they would attach themselves to and pursue those who neglected to pay them the proper attention, whom they wished to avenge, or whom they had some reason to hate.

Some of the foregoing stories bear a strong resemblance to the stories of Incubi and Succubi sprinkled through ancient literature. Incubi are the forms of men who attach themselves to women, and Succubi the forms of women who attach themselves to men, with the result that their caresses lead often to strangling. Nicholas Ramy relates in his *Demonolatrie*

that a Lorraine shepherd, named Pierron, a
married man, with a son of from eight to
ten years of age, conceived a violent love
for a girl in the village.   One day, when he
was thinking of this girl, she appeared
before him, or rather, a demon under her
figure.   Pierron avowed his love ; she was
willing to respond, but on condition that
he should submit to her in all things.   The
shepherd consented and took his pleasures
with the spectre, with disastrous results.
Servius Tullius, King of the Romans,
according to some ancient authors, was
the son of a slave and of Vulcan, according
to others, of a salamander, and according
to the demonographers, of an incubus.
According to Rabbi Elias, Adam for one
hundred years was visited by female
demons, who, through him, were delivered
of demons, lamies, spectres, and evil
phantoms.   Hector de Boethius, in his
History of Scotland, records that a young
man of great beauty was pursued by a
young demon who crossed his threshold
and offered to espouse herself to him.   He
complained to his bishop, who ordered him
to fast, pray, and confess, whereupon he
ceased to be troubled by the spirit.

CHAPTER X

MISCELLANEA

VOLTAIRE was surprised that in the enlightened eighteenth century there should still be people found who believed in the reality of vampires, and that the doctors of the Sorbonne should give their *imprimatur* to a dissertation on these unpleasant creatures. Yet from 1730 to 1735 the subject of vampirism formed a principal topic of conversation, and may be said to have been a mania all over the world, with Europe as a particular centre. Pamphlets on the subject streamed from the press, the newspapers vied with one another in recording fresh achievements of the spectres, and though the philosophers scoffed at and ridiculed the belief, yet sovereigns sent officers and commissioners to report upon their misdeeds. The favourite scenes of their exploits were Hungary, Poland, Silesia, Bohemia, and Moravia, and in those countries a vampire haunted and tormented almost every village.

In some parts of Scandinavia a singular method was adopted for getting rid of vampires, viz. by instituting judicial proceedings against them. Inhabitants were regularly summoned to attend the inquest; a tribunal was constituted; charges were preferred with the usual legal formalities, accusing them of molesting the houses and introducing death among the inhabitants; and at the end of the proceedings judgment was proclaimed. The priest then entered with holy water, Mass was celebrated, and it was held that complete conquest had been gained over the goblins.

Sir Walter Scott, in his translation of *Eyrbyggia Saga*, relates a traditional story of several vampires who committed dreadful ravages in Iceland in the year 1000, so that in a household of thirty servants no less than eighteen died.

Saxo Grammaticus, the earliest chronicler and writer upon Danish history and folklore, in his *Danish History* (book i.), dealing with the origin of the Danes, relates the following story :—

One Mith-othin, who was famous for his juggling tricks, was quickened, as though by an inspiration from on High, to seize the opportunity of feigning to be a god ; and, wrapping the minds of the barbarians in fresh darkness, he led them by the renown of his jugglings to pay holy observance to his name. He said that the wrath of the gods could never be appeased nor the outrage to their deity expiated by mixed and indiscriminate sacrifices, and, therefore, forbade that prayers for this end should be put up without distinction, appointing to each of those above his especial drink-offering. But when Odin was returning, he cast away all help of jugglings, went to Finland to hide himself, and was there attacked and slain by the inhabitants. Even in his death his abominations were made manifest, for those who came nigh his barrow were cut off by a kind of sudden death ; and, after his end, he spread such pestilence that he seemed almost to leave a filthier record in his death than in his life ; it was as though he would extort from the guilty a punishment for his slaughter. The inhabitants being in this trouble, took the body out of the mound, beheaded it, and impaled it through the breast with a sharp stake, and herein that people found relief.

In book ii. we have the story of Aswid and Asmund. Aswid died and was buried with horse and dog. Asmund died and was buried with his friend, food being provided for him to eat. Later on the grave opened, when Asmund appeared and said: "By some strange enterprise of the power of hell the spirit of Aswid was sent up from the nether world, and with cruel tooth eats the fleet-footed (horse) and has given his dog to his abominable jaws. Not sated with devouring the horse or hound, he soon turned his swift nails upon me, tearing my cheek and taking off my ear. Hence the hideous sight of my slashed countenance, the blood spurts in the ugly wound. Yet the bringer of horrors did it not unscathed; for soon I cut off his head with my steel, and impaled his guilty carcase with a stake."

In Malaysia the vampires are mostly females, and are credited with a great

fondness for fish. They are known as
Langsuirs, and Skeat, in *Malay Magic*, gives
the following charm for " laying " a Lang-
suir :—

O ye mosquito-fry at the river's mouth,
When yet a great way off ye are sharp of eye;
When near, ye are hard of heart.
When the rock in the ground opens of itself,
Then (and then only) be emboldened the hearts of my
    foes and opponents !
When the corpse in the ground opens of itself,
Then (and then only) be emboldened the hearts of my
    foes and opponents !
May your heart be softened when you behold me,
By grace of this prayer that I use, called Silam Bayn.

Abercromby, in his work on the Finns,
says that the Ceremis imagine that the
spirits that cause illness, especially fever
and ague, are continually recruited on the
death of old maids, murderers, and those
that die a violent death. Whenever anyone becomes dangerously ill, the Lapps feel
sure that one of his deceased relatives wants
his company in the region of the dead,
either from affection or to punish him for
some trespass. The Truks of Altai have
a similar belief. The soul after death
willingly lingers for some time in the house
and leaves it unwillingly, and often takes

with it some other members of the family
or some of the cattle.

Codrington, in his descriptive work on
the Melanesians, says that there is a belief
in Banks Islands in the existence of a
power like that of vampires. A man or a
woman would obtain this power out of
a morbid desire for communion with some
ghost, and in order to gain it would steal
and eat a morsel of a corpse. The ghost
of the dead man would then join in a close
friendship with the person who had eaten,
and would gratify him by afflicting anyone
against whom his ghostly power might be
directed. The man so afflicted would feel
that something was influencing his life, and
would come to dread some particular person
among his neighbours, who was, therefore,
suspected of being a *talamur*. This name
was also given to one whose soul was
supposed to leave the grave and absorb the
lingering vitality of a freshly dead corpse.
There was a woman, some years ago, of
whom the story is told that she made no
secret of doing this, and that once on the
death of a neighbour she gave notice that
she would go in the night and eat the
corpse. The friends of the deceased there-

fore kept watch in the house where the corpse lay, and at dead of night heard a scratching at the door, followed by a rustling noise close by the corpse. One of them threw a stone and seemed to hit the unknown thing; and in the morning the *talamur* was found with a bruise on her arm, which she confessed was caused by a stone thrown at her while she was eating the corpse.

Baron von Haxthausen, in his work on Transcaucasia, tells us that there once dwelt in a cavern in Armenia a vampire called Dakhanavar, who could not endure anyone to penetrate into the mountains of Ulmish Altotem or count their valleys. Everyone who attempted this had in the night his blood sucked by the monster from the soles of his feet until he died. The vampire was, however, at last outwitted by two cunning fellows. They began to count the valleys, and when night came on they lay down to sleep—taking care to place themselves with the feet of the one under the head of the other. In the night the monster came, felt as usual, and found a head; then he felt at the other end and found a head there also. "Well," cried he,

"I have gone through the whole 366
valleys of these mountains, and have sucked
the blood of people without end, but never
yet did I come across anyone with two
heads and no feet!" So saying, he ran
away and was never more seen in that
country, but ever after the people knew that
the mountain has 366 valleys.

Even America is not free from the belief
in the vampire. In one of the issues of the
Norwich (U.S.A.) *Courier* for 1854, there
is the account of an incident that occurred
at Jewett, a city in that vicinity. About
eight years previously, Horace Ray of Gris-
wold had died of consumption. Afterwards,
two of his children—grown-up sons—died
of the same disease, the last one dying about
1852. Not long before the date of the news-
paper the same fatal disease had seized
another son, whereupon it was determined
to exhume the bodies of the two brothers
and burn them, because the dead were
supposed to feed upon the living; and so
long as the dead body in the grave
remained undecomposed, either wholly
or in part, the surviving members of the
family must continue to furnish substance
on which the dead body could feed. Acting

under the influence of this strange superstition, the family and friends of the deceased proceeded to the burial-ground on
June 8th, 1854, dug up the bodies of the
deceased brothers, and burned them on
the spot.

Dr Dyer, an eminent physician of Chicago,
also reported in 1875 a case occurring
within his own personal knowledge, where
the body of a woman who had died of
consumption was taken from her grave
and her lungs burned, under the belief that
she was drawing after her into the grave
some of her surviving relatives. In 1874,
according to the *Providence Journal*, in the
village of Placedale, Rhode Island, Mr
William Rose dug up the body of his own
daughter and burned her heart, under the
belief that she was draining the vitality of
other members of the family.

The vampire is not an unknown spectre
in China, where the measures adopted for
the riddance of the pest are generally the
burning of the mortal remains of the corpse,
or removing to a distance the lid of the
coffin after the vampire has started on his
nocturnal rounds. It is held that the air
thus entering freely into the coffin will

cause the contents to decay. Another
Chinese cure for vampires is to watch any
suspected coffin until the corpse has quitted
it, and then strew rice, red peas, and bits of
iron around it. The corpse, on returning,
will find it impossible to pass over these
things, and will thus fall an easy prey to
his captors.

The following story of a Chinese vampire
is related by Dr J. J. M. de Groot in his
Religious System of China (vol. v. p. 747):—

"Liu N. N., a literary graduate of the
lowest degree in Wukiang (in Kiangsu),
was in charge of some pupils belonging to
the Tsaing family in the Yuen-hwo district.
In the season of Pure Brightness he returned
home, some holidays being granted him to
sweep his ancestral tombs. This duty
performed, he returned to his post, and
said to his wife : ' To-morrow I must go ;
cook some food for me at an early hour.'
The woman said she would do so, and rose
for the purpose at cockcrow. Their village
lay on the hill behind their dwelling, facing
a brook. The wife washed some rice at the
brook, picked some vegetables in the garden,
and had everything ready, but when it was
light her husband did not rise. She went

into his room to wake him up, but however
often she called he gave no answer. She
then drew the curtains and found him
lying across the bed, headless, though not
a trace of blood could be seen.

" Terror-stricken, she called the neighbours. All of them suspected her of adultery
with a lover, and murder, and they warned
the magistrate. This grandee came and
held a preliminary inquest ; he ordered the
corpse to be coffined, had the woman put
in fetters, and examined her ; so he put her
in gaol, and many months passed away
without sentence being pronounced. Then
a neighbour, coming uphill for some fuel,
saw a neglected grave with a coffin lid bare ;
it was quite a sound coffin, strong and solid,
and yet the lid was raised a little ; so he
naturally suspected that it had been opened
by thieves. He summoned the people ;
they lifted the lid off and saw a corpse with
features like a living person and a body
covered with white hair. Between its arms
it held the head of a man, which they
recognised as that of Liu, the graduate.
They reported the case to the magistrate ;
the coroners ordered the head to be taken
away, but it was so firmly grasped in the

arms of the corpse that the combined
efforts of a number of men proved in-
sufficient to draw it out. So the magistrate
told them to chop off the arms of the
kiangshi (corpse - spectre). Fresh blood
gushed out of the wounds, but in Liu's head
there was not a drop left, it having been
sucked dry by the monster. By magis-
terial order the corpse was burned, and the
case ended with the release of the woman
from gaol."

An account of the following is to be
found in various works, including the
fragments of Phlegon, who was liberated
from captivity by the Emperor Hadrian :—

A citizen of Ætolia, named Polycrite,
was elected by the people to govern the
country because of his probity and talents.
While in enjoyment of this dignity he
married a woman of Locris, whom he
courted and espoused in the hope of being
happy ; but he died suddenly on the fourth
night of the nuptials, leaving his wife
pregnant with an hermaphrodite, which
was born nine months afterwards. The
priests and augurs having been consulted
on this prodigy, conjectured that the
Ætolians and Locrians would go to war

because of the fact that the monster had two natures. In order that they might prevent this evil, they decided to conduct the mother and her child outside the boundaries of Ætolia and there burn them both. The sacrificers and the victims formed up into a procession, accompanied by a great crowd of people. But as they were about to carry the sentence into effect, the spectre of Polycrite appeared on the pyre and, robed in a black gown, stood near to his child. The frightened spectators sought to take refuge in flight, but he recalled them and assured them that there was nothing to fear, and then, in a deep bass voice, he delivered a discourse in which he told his compatriots that if they burnt his wife and child they would suffer very great calamities. Seeing, however, that, despite his remonstrances, the Ætolians were determined to carry out their resolution, this spectre thereupon seized his offspring, and, living as he was, tore him to pieces and devoured him. The people called out with horror and threw stones at him in order to drive him away. He took little notice of these insults, braving the stones, and continued his unholy feast, devouring all but the head, when he vanished from sight. This incident seemed so dreadful, that the people wished to consult the Delphic oracle, when the head of the child spoke and predicted a number of evils that should fall on the Ætolians.

Debonnair, in his *Histoire de France*, says that when the Huns went to attack Caribert, eighth King of France, those barbarians brought with them a formidable force composed of the spectres of their ancestors, against whom the French were compelled to fight. An old chronicle adds that these spectres in combat seized the living by the throat and strangled them. Nevertheless, the French gained the victory. When Charles-le-Chauve besieged Angers, some evil spirits under the forms of *sauterelles*, with very large thumbs, assailed the French army. The soldiers were unable to extricate themselves from these enemies except by exorcisms, when they were driven towards the sea. Thomas Bartholin assures us that the ancient Danish frequently fought with spectres, with which their country was infested. The sedate Melanchthon relates

11

that his aunt was disabled by a treacherous touch from her deceased husband, who burnt her hand while holding it.

Michael Raufft, a German writer, says that some of the dead devour the cloths and everything within their reach except ing only their own flesh; but in some parts of Germany it is frequently a custom to place in the coffin a small portion of earth under the chin, sometimes a piece of silver and a stone in the mouth, or else they tightly close the mouth with a handkerchief.

Miss J. A. Middleton, in her work, *Another Grey Ghost Book*, relates the following story, which she came across in manuscript :—

" A French viscount—de Morière by name—was one of the very few French noblemen who managed to retain their estates through the troublous times of the French Revolution. He was an extraordinary-looking man, very tall and thin, with a high, almost pointed, forehead, and protruding teeth.

" Under an air of suave courtesy and kindness he concealed a ferociously cruel disposition, which showed itself when the

fires of the great revolution had burned
themselves out, and all was once more
quiet. To get level, as it were, with the
working classes, he sent for his retainers
and workpeople one by one, and, after
he had interviewed them, cut off their
heads. It is not surprising to hear that,
in return, he himself met his death by
assassination at the hands of some of
the peasantry.

" No sooner, however, was the viscount
laid in the grave than an appalling number
of young children died in the neighbourhood, all of whom bore vampire marks
at their throats. Later on, when he had
been buried for some time, and while the
tomb was being repaired, there were nine
more cases in a single week. The awful
slaughter went on until seventy-two years
passed away, and the viscount's grandson
succeeded to the title.

" Young de Morième, hearing the appalling stories of h's grandfather, consulted a
priest with the idea of laying his horrible
ancestor's ghost, and, after some dis-
cussion and delay, it was decided to open
the tomb. The services of a man specially
successful in such cases were obtained,

and the vault was opened in the presence of the authorities.

"Every coffin was found to have undergone the usual process of rotting away, except that of the old viscount, which, after seventy-two years, was perfectly sound and strong. The lid was removed and the body was found quite fresh and free from decomposition. The face was flushed and there was blood in the heart and chest. The skin was soft and natural. New nails had grown on both hands and feet.

"The body was removed from the coffin and a white thorn was driven by the expert through the heart of the corpse, with the ghastly result that blood and water poured forth and the corpse groaned and screamed. Then the remains were burned on the seashore; and from that day the child-deaths ceased and there were no more mysterious crimes in the neighbourhood.

"The family archives were searched and it was found that the old viscount had come originally from Persia, where he married an Indian wife, and afterwards took up his residence in France, where he became a naturalised subject. The vampiric taint was in his blood."

Another case Miss Middleton heard of was that of a man who became vampirish through being bitten by a vampire bat. There are two kinds of these creatures, both of which frequent the tropics. Darwin himself, who spoke of the credulity with which such cannibalism was regarded in England, caught one of these bats in the act of sucking the blood from a horse and put the incident on record.

Fischer says that the bite of a vampire leaves, in general, no mark upon the person. But, he adds, " it is nevertheless speedily fatal," unless the bitten person protects himself by eating some of the earth from the grave of the vampire and smearing himself with his blood ; but, unfortunately, these measures are seldom, if ever, of more than temporary use. Fischer then adds : " If through these precautions the life of the victim be prolonged for a period, sooner or later he ends with becoming a vampire himself ; that is to say, he dies and is buried, but continues to lead a vampire life in the grave, nourishing himself by infecting others, and promiscuously propagating vampirism."

E. P. Evans, in his interesting work on the *Criminal Prosecution and Capital Punishment of Animals,* relates that in 1337 a herdsman near the town of Cadan came forth from his grave every night, visiting the villages, terrifying the inhabitants, conversing affably with some, and murdering others. Every person, however, with whom he associated was doomed to die within eight days and to wander as a vampire after death. In order to keep him in his grave, a stake was driven through his body, but he only laughed at this clumsy attempt to impale a ghost, saying, " You have really rendered me a great service by providing me with a staff with which to ward off the dogs when I go out for a walk." At length it was decided to hand him over to the two public executioners to be burned, and it is averred that when the fire began to take effect, " he drew up his feet, bellowed for a while like a bull, and he-hawed like an ass, until one of the executioners stabbed him in the side, so that the blood oozed out, and the evil finally ceased."

Again, in 1345, in the town of Lewin,
a potter's wife, who was reputed to be a
witch, died, and, owing to suspicions of
her pact with Satan, was refused burial
in consecrated ground and dumped into
a ditch like a dog. The after-events
proved that she was not a good Christian,
for, instead of remaining quietly in her
grave, such as it was, she roamed about
in the form of divers unclean beasts,
causing much terror and slaying sundry
persons. Thereupon her body was exhumed, and it was found that she had
chewed and swallowed one-half of her
face-cloth, which on being pulled out of
her throat showed stains of blood. A
stake was driven through her breast, but
this only seemed to make matters worse.
She now walked abroad with the stake in
her hand and killed quite a number of
people with this formidable weapon. Her
body was then taken up a second time
and burned, whereupon she ceased from
troubling. The efficacy of this post-
mortem *auto-da-fé* was accepted as conclusive proof that her neighbours had
neglected to perform their whole religious
duty in not having burned her when she

was alive, and they had been thus punished for their remissness.

Döpler also cites the case of Stephen Hubner, of Trautenau, who wandered after death as a vampire frightening and strangling several individuals. By order of the Court, his body was disinterred and decapitated under the gallows-tree. When his head was struck off, a stream of blood spurted forth, although he had been already five months buried. His remains were reduced to ashes, and nothing more was heard of him.

In 1573, the Parliament of Dôle published a decree, permitting the inhabitants of the Franche-Comté to pursue and kill a were-wolf or loup-garou, which infested that province, "notwithstanding the existing laws concerning the chase." The people were empowered to "assemble with javelins, halberds, pikes, arquebuses and clubs, to hunt and pursue the said were-wolf in all places where they could find it, and to take, burn, and kill it, without incurring any fine or other penalty." The hunt seems to have been successful, if we may judge from the fact that the same tribunal in the following year condemned

to be burned a man named Giles Garnier,
who ran on all fours in the forest and fields
and devoured little children, " even on
Friday." The poor lycanthrope, it appears,
had as slight respect for ecclesiastical fasts
as the French pig, which was not restrained
by any feeling of piety from eating infants
on a fast day.

Philip Rehrius, in the seventeenth
century, and Michel Raufft, at the
commencement of the eighteenth, even
published treatises on the dead who ate
in their sepulchres — *De masticatione
mortuorum in tumulis.*

Miss J. A. Middleton (*Another Grey
Ghost Book*) says that the people who
mostly become vampires are witches,
wizards, suicides, those who have been
cursed, and those who have met with
violent deaths. There is also, she says,
a prevalent idea that the illegitimate sons
of parents who are themselves illegitimate,
are peculiarly liable to become vampirised.

At a village a few leagues from Barlaw,
in Moldavia, there died in February 1729
an aged gardener, feared throughout the
neighbourhood, where he was believed to
be a sorcerer. During the night which

preceded his interment his body, which was placed in the church, was moved from its place, and the black cloth which covered it was stolen ; however, on the following morning, the body was found in the coffin exactly as it had been placed there. The facts were not published at the time, but his interment was hastened, but before placing him in the ground a stone was placed in his mouth. Three nights after the funeral a young woman of the village, betrothed and on the point of marrying, was frightened beyond description and quitted her bed, pursued by a horrible phantom. She hastened to her friends and told them that the old gardener had come into her bedroom and said to her : " I have come to suck from you, as I have already sucked from him who is to be your husband," and, at the same time, had seized her by the throat. She added that she had been awakened by her struggle with the vampire. Instead of assuring her that what she had seen was only a vision, her relatives, as frightened as she was, told the neighbours of the incident and demanded the exhumation of the gardener's remains. However, the young

woman died two days after the occurrence.
It was ascertained that her betrothed
husband had not seen the vampire nor
had he suffered from him in any way.
He was, however, told that the spectre
had said that he, too, would fall ill and
die eight days after his fiancée, which
really happened. Then the gardener's
body was exhumed, and, being found to
be of a fresh colour, it was duly burned.

John Brompton relates in his *Chronicles*
that St Augustine, the apostle of England,
after having preached a sermon on the
duty of paying the tithe, then called out,
as was customary before commencing mass :
" Let no one under excommunication assist
at the Holy Sacrifice ! " He immediately
saw leave the church a dead man who
had been buried for a hundred and fifty
years. After mass was concluded, St
Augustine, preceded by the Cross, went
and asked the dead man why he had left
the church. The deceased answered that
it was because he had died whilst under
sentence of excommunication. The saint
asked him at once to say where the priest
who had excommunicated him was buried.
Together they went to the spot, and St

Augustine called upon the priest to arise. He returned to life, and, in reply to St Augustine's question, said that his principal reason for excommunicating the man was because he had refused to pay the tithe. On the supplication of the saint, however, he gave absolution to the sinner, and the two men then returned to rest in their tombs. Brompton's narrative has been reproduced by Calmet, Simmonet, and other writers.

At the latter end of August 1923 (see *Observer*, 2nd September 1923) it was claimed that a vampire ventured into the Serbian capital, Belgrade, and gave vent to its feelings by throwing stones at the house of its victim. Bricks and fragments of big stones fell day after day on No. 61 Bosanska Street, which runs from the old " Gates of the Town," near the railway station, into the picturesque Balkanska Street. All the windows of the house were broken, and the terrified inhabitants barricaded the house with packing-cases, tables, and chairs. The older inhabitants perambulated the yard of the house, sprinkling holy water and chanting psalms and hymns, but it is not on record whether the vampire was captured and transfixed with the customary briar stake.

The "asasabonsam," to which Mr Sutherland Rattray has drawn attention in his *Ashanti Proverbs*, is a monster of human shape, which lives far in the depths of the forest and is only occasionally met by hunters. It sits on tree-tops, and its legs dangle down to the ground and have hooks for feet which pick up anyone who comes within reach. It has iron teeth and is of both male and female species. Mr Sutherland Rattray also refers to the " obayifo," derived from *bayi*, " sorcery," which is a kind of human vampire whose chief delight is to suck the blood of children, whereby the latter pine and die. Men and women possessed of this power are credited with volitant powers, with being able to quit their bodies and travel great distances in the night. Besides sucking the blood of their victims, they are supposed to be able to extract the sap and juices of crops, and cases of coco blight are ascribed to them. These people are supposed to be very common, and a man never knows but that his friend or even his wife may be one. When prowling at night they are supposed to emit a phosphorescent light. An obayifo in everyday life is supposed to be known by having sharp, shifty eyes, that are never at rest, also by showing an undue interest in food.

A few months since an incident occurred in Bosnia which proves that the belief in vampires and evil spirits still prevails there. In the village of Tupanjari, two peasant brothers, in company with ten of their neighbours, opened the grave of their recently buried father at midnight, took out the body and burned it. Then they put the ashes in the coffin and replaced the coffin in the grave. The utmost secrecy was maintained for some time, but eventually the gendarmes heard of what had happened and arrested the brothers. They confessed their guilt, but pleaded that they had acted at the instigation of their mother. On the night after the funeral of their father, they said, his ghost had come to the house and had prevented their mother from sleeping. Afterwards the ghost came again, and robbed the whole family of their sleep. They feared that it would disturb the whole village, and therefore resolved to burn the body, and did so with the aid of ten neighbours, because, according to local tradition, not fewer than twelve persons must perform the act. Since then the ghost had not reappeared. The mayor thereupon solemnly declared that the only possible way of rendering a vampire harmless was by burning him, and as the dead man had become a vampire, the only thing to do was to burn the body.

CHAPTER XI

THE living vampire is regarded as distinct and separate from the dead species. In Epirus and Thessaly there is a belief in living vampires, who leave their shepherd dwellings by night and roam about, biting and tearing men and animals and sucking their blood. In Moldavia and in Wallachia, the *murony* are real, living men who become dogs at night, with the backbone prolonged to form a sort of tail. They roam through the villages, and their main delight is to kill cattle.

In some countries the belief prevails that the soul of a living man, usually a sorcerer, leaves its proper body asleep and goes forth, perhaps in the visible form of a straw or fluff of down, slips through the keyholes, and attacks its sleeping victim. If the sleeper should wake in time to clutch this tiny soul-embodiment, he may through it have his revenge by maltreating or destroying its bodily owner.

The following account was contributed by me to the *Occult Review* for July 1910. The particulars are given exactly as I wrote them down in shorthand from the narrator's dictation. My informant is a well-known medical practitioner in the West End of London, who has held various official appointments in the tropics, and I received his assurance that the incidents recorded happened exactly as they are described. Whether the Indian referred to is still alive or not is unknown, but certainly the two other principals, at the time of writing, are.

Some years ago a small number of English officials were stationed in a small place in the tropics. Their residences were about a quarter of a mile from each other, three of the bungalows standing in their own compounds and on separate elevations. Suddenly one of the officials fell ill, but the district medical officer was quite unable to trace the cause of the illness. The official in question made several applications to the Colonial Office for transfer to another station, saying he felt he should die if he remained there. At first the application was refused, but the man got worse and fell into a very depressed mental condition. He eventually wrote again, saying that if his application for transfer could not be granted he would be compelled to throw up his appointment—a serious matter for him, as he had no private means. The application was then granted; he was transferred, and he recovered his health.

About eighteen months later another official had a slight attack of fever, from which he fully recovered; but after this attack he began to complain of lassitude until he went beyond a certain distance from his residence. The moment he returned to within this distance he said he felt as though a wet blanket had been thrown over him, and nothing could rouse him from the depression which seized him. He, too, fell into a low state of health, and on his request was transferred to another station.

Shortly after this transfer the wife of the district medical officer, living within the same area, began to fail in health and became terribly depressed, apparently from no cause whatever. Previously she had been a cheerful, happy woman, indulging in games and outdoor sports of all kinds, but now she became most depressed and miserable. At last, one night, about twelve o'clock, she woke up shrieking. Her husband rushed into her room, and she said she had woken up with a most awful feeling of depression, and had seen a creature travelling along the cornice of the room. She could only describe it as having a resemblance to something between a gigantic spider and a huge jelly-fish. Her husband ascribed it to an attack of nightmare, but he was disturbed in the same manner on the following night, when his wife said she had been awake for a quarter of an hour, but had not had the strength to call him before. He found her in a state of collapse, her pulse exceedingly weak, her temperature three degrees below normal, and her body in a cold sweat. He mixed her a draught which had the effect of sending her to sleep.

In the morning she said she must leave the station and go home, as to stop there would mean her death. Thinking to divert her attention, her husband took her away on a pleasure trip, when he was glad to see that she entirely recovered her former cheerful expression and high spirits. This state of things lasted until, returning home in a rickshaw alongside her husband's, her face changed and she resumed her gloomy countenance.

" There," she said, " is it not awful ? I have been so well and happy all the week, and now I feel as though a pall had been thrown over me."

Matters got worse, and she became more depressed than ever, and only a few nights passed before her husband was again called to her bedside about midnight. He found his wife in a state of considerable weakness, although it was not so acute as on the previous occasion. She said to him : " I want you to examine the back of my neck and shoulders very carefully and see if there is any mark on the skin of any kind whatever."

Her husband did so, but could not find a mark.

" Get a glass and look again. See if you can find any puncture from a sharp-pointed tooth."

He made a microscopical examination, but found absolutely nothing.

" Now," said his wife, " I can tell you what is the matter. I dreamed that I was in a house where I lived when I was a girl. My little boy called out to me. I ran down to him, but when I reached the bottom of the stairs a tall, black man came towards me. I waved him off, but I could not move to get away from him, though I pushed the boy out of his reach. The man came towards me, seized me in his arms, sat down at the bottom of the stairs, put me on his knee, and proceeded to suck from a point at the upper part of the spine, just below the neck. I felt that he was drawing all the blood and life out of me. Then he threw me from him, and apparently I lost consciousness as he did so. I felt as though I was dying. Then I woke up, and I had been lying here for a quarter of an hour or twenty minutes before I was able to call you."

" Have you ever experienced anything of this character before ? " asked her husband.

" No, I have not ; but night after night for many months I have woken up in exactly the same state, and that has been the sole cause of my mental depression. I have not said anything about it because it seemed so foolish, but now I have had this definite dream I cannot hold my tongue any longer."

She soon passed into a peaceful sleep, and on discussing the matter the following morning with her husband she said : " I have a feeling somehow that it will not happen again.   I feel quite well and strong, and all my depression is gone."

In the afternoon husband and wife were going together to the club, when around the corner of the jungle came a tall Indian, the owner of a large number of milch cattle, and reputed to be a wealthy man.   The surgeon's wife suddenly stopped, turned pale, and said immediately : " That is the man I saw in my dream."

The husband went directly up to the man and said to him : " Look here, I will give you twelve hours to get out of this place.   I know everything that happened last night at midnight, and I will kill you like a dog if I find you here in twelve hours' time."

The Indian disappeared the same night, taking with him only a few valuables and a little loose money.   He left behind him

the money that was deposited in the bank,
as well as the whole of his property. His
forty head of cattle, worth eighty dollars
each, were impounded, and no news had
been heard of him five years afterwards.
Since his departure no one has complained
of depression and lassitude in that area.

In 1922 a commission of doctors appointed by the Soviet Government discovered three hundred cases of cannibalism.
One man owned up to killing sixteen persons.
The commission reported that cannibalism
occurs among young persons (nearly always
women and young girls), who dig up corpses
in cemeteries; and those, chiefly degenerate,
who kill in order to eat the bodies. It was
also asserted that cannibalism had dimin-
ished since the Government had left the duty
of punishment to the people themselves.

In 1849 a striking and appalling instance
of insanity occupied the attention of the
French psychologists. It was communi-
cated to the *Journal of Psychological Medicine* by Dr G. Sigmond, formerly Professor
of Materia Medica to the Royal Medico-
Botanical Society and Lecturer on Medical
Jurisprudence at the Grosvenor School,
St George's Hospital, London. In July

1849 Sergeant Bertrand was charged before
the Council of War of the Department
of the Seine (Paris being at that time
under military law) with breaking into
cemeteries, dragging from their graves and
savagely mutilating bodies recently interred. The mutilations of the bodies had
been with the object of covering his crime,
which was that of cohabitation with the
dead. He stated in his confession that
when he disinterred the corpse of a man he
felt loathing and disgust, but when that of
a female presented itself, he rushed upon
it with avidity and ardour. He satisfied
a deplorable passion and then fell into a
state of convulsive stupor. He lay down
upon the ground in the open air amongst
the shrubs, even in the most incle-
ment weather. He remained in a lethargy
unconscious of all that passed around
him, and for several hours seemed lost to
every earthly feeling. The repulsive story
seemed borne out by all the facts that
were produced, and the man's admission
was looked upon as conclusive evidence.
The court declared him guilty of a mis-
demeanour, for which the most severe
punishment under the Code Napoleon was

twelve months' imprisonment, which sentence was passed.

Georget, in his *Examen Médical des Procès Criminels*, cites the case of Leger, an old soldier, who was tried in the year 1824 by the Court of Assizes at Versailles. The accused had seized a little girl at the entrance of the forest, murdered her, sucked her blood, violated her, torn out her heart, and mutilated her bosom and her sexual organs, besides eating some portion of her flesh. Upon his trial, he wore an air of gaiety and satisfaction, until he heard the melancholy evidence of the poor girl's mother, when he burst into tears, and with much apparent sympathy exclaimed : " I am, indeed, sorry to have deprived you of your daughter. I implore your pardon." Georget, who examined the case minutely after the man had been condemned to death (which sentence he heard with perfect indifference), says of him : " He was not, as has generally been said, a great criminal, a monster, a cannibal, a man-eater, who wished to renew the feast of Atreus ; this individual was, in my opinion, an unfortunate imbecile, a madman, who ought to have been confined as a lunatic."

CHAPTER XII

THE subject of vampirism does not appear to have attracted litterateurs greatly. True, there are the operas of Palma, Hart, Marschner, and von Lindpainter; and Philostratus and Phlegon of Tralles have discoursed upon the phenomena. There are not, however, many works of fiction based upon the topic, or many poems in which the subject is introduced. There is an Anglo-Saxon poem with the title *A Vampyre of the Fens*, and a long, wearisome novel, full of gruesome details, entitled *Varney the Vampire*. Among modern authors, Mr Bram Stoker has made the vampire the foundation of his exciting romance *Dracula*, and Mr Reginald Hodder has written a romance entitled *The Vampire*, to which I allude on a later page. Mention of these works almost exhausts the references upon the subject.

Nor are the references to vampires and

vampirism in the ancient Greek authors
more numerous. The phantom of Achilles
is represented by Euripides (*Hec.*, 109,
599) as appearing on his tomb clad in
golden armour and appeased by the sacrifice of a young virgin, whose blood he drank.
Œdipus also in Sophocles (*Œd. Col.*, 621),
when foretelling a defeat which the Thebans
would sustain near his tomb, declares that
his cold, dead body will drink their warm
blood. Human victims were offered at the
funeral pyre of Patroclus as we find in the
Iliad (vol. i.).

Though human beings are not mentioned
as being sacrificed in the *Odyssey*, yet the
blood of slaughtered sheep was eagerly
lapped up by the ghosts consulted by
Odysseus (xi. 45, 48, 95, 96, 153, etc.). A
sheep was also to be sacrificed at the tombs
of mortals, and its blood was supposed to be
an offering acceptable to the departed spirit.

Pausanias, Strabo, Ælian, and Suidas
relate the legend of Ulysses in his wander-
ings coming to the town of Temesa, in Italy,
where one of his associates was stoned to
death by the townsmen for having ravished
a virgin. His ghost forthwith haunted
the inhabitants, and caused them such

annoyance that many were thinking seriously of leaving the town when they were
told by Apollo's oracle that to appease
him they must build the hero a temple,
and sacrifice to him yearly the most beautiful virgin they had among them. The
temple was accordingly raised : access to
the sacred enclosure was prohibited to all
except the priests, on penalty of death. An
engraving of the evil spirit that is alleged
to have infested Temesa is given on page
18 of Beaumont's *Treatise on Spirits* (ed.
1705).

Philostratus, in his *Life of Apollonius of
Tyana* (iv. 25, p. 165), says that the long
intercourse which took place between a
female spectre and the Corinthian Menip-
pus was but a prelude to the feast of flesh
and blood in which she meant to revel
after their marriage.

Some have described the Hebrew *lilith*
as a vampire, but the *Jewish Encyclopædia*
states that : " There is nothing in the
Talmud to indicate that the *lilith* was a
vampire." She was regarded as a nocturnal demon, flying about in the form of a
night-owl, and stealing children, and was
held to have permission to kill all children

sinfully begotten, even from a lawful wife.
The *lilith* is held to have the same signifi-
cation as the Greek *strigæ* and *lamiæ*, who
were sorceresses or magicians, seeking to
put to death new-born children. The
ancient Greeks believed that these *lamiæ*
devoured children, or sucked away all their
blood until they died. Euripides and the
scholiast of Aristophanes mention the *lilith*
as a dangerous monster, the enemy of
mortals; and Ovid describes the *strigæ* as
dangerous birds, which fly by night and
seek for infants to devour them and nourish
themselves with their blood. The *aluka*
of Proverbs xxx. 15 is more akin to the
vampire. It is a blood-sucking, insatiable
monster; the word is synonymous with
algul, the well-known demon of the Arabian
popular stories, "the man-devouring demon
of the waste," known as the ghoul or goule
in the translated edition of the *Arabian
Nights*.

Goethe, in his ballad *The Bride of Corinth*,
describes how a young Athenian visits a
friend of his father, to whose daughter he
had been betrothed, and is disturbed at
midnight by the appearance of the vampire
spectre of her whom death has prevented

from becoming his bride, and who, when detected, says :—

> From my grave to wander I am forc'd,
>   Still to seek The Good's long-sever'd link,
> Still to love the bridegroom I have lost,
>   And the life-blood of his heart to drink ;
>   When his race is run,
>   I must hasten on,
> And the young must 'neath my vengeance sink.

There is one scant reference to the subject in Shelley's poems. Byron, in his poem *The Giaour*, has the following passage :—

> But first on earth as vampire sent
> Thy corse shall from its tomb be rent :
> Then ghastly haunt thy native place,
> And suck the blood of all thy race.

Dryden relates :—

> Lo, in my walks where wicked elves have been,
> The learning of the parish now is seen—
> From fiends and imps he sets the village free,
> There haunts not any incubus but he :
> The maids and women need no danger fear
> To walk by night and sanctity so near.

Scott, in *Rokeby*, has the following lines :—

> For like the bat of Indian brakes,
> Her pinions fan the wound she makes,
> And soothing thus the dreamer's pains,
> She drinks the life-blood from the veins.

The following legend is related in vol. ii. of *Minstrelsy of the Scottish Border*, and is referred to in a footnote to Southey's *Thalaba the Destroyer* (p. 108, ed. 1814) :—

In the year 1058 a young man of noble birth had been married in Rome, and during the period of his nuptial feast, having gone with his companions to play at ball, he put his marriage ring on the finger of a broken statue of Venus in the area, to remain while he was engaged in recreation. Desisting from the exercise, he found the finger on which he had put his ring contracted firmly against the palm, and attempted in vain either to break or disengage the ring. He concealed the circumstances from his companions, and returned at night with a servant, when he found the finger extended and the ring gone. He dissembled the loss and returned to his wife ; but when he attempted to embrace her he found himself prevented by something dark and dense, which was tangible if not visible, intervening between them ; and he heard a voice saying : " Embrace me ! for I am Venus, whom this day you wedded, and I will not restore your ring." As this was constantly repeated, he consulted his relatives, who had recourse to Palumbus, the priest, skilled in necromancy. He directed the young man to go at a certain hour of the night to a spot among the ruins of ancient Rome where four roads meet, and wait silently till he saw a company pass by, and then, without uttering a word, to deliver a letter which he gave him to a majestic being who rode in a chariot after the rest of the company. The young man did as he was directed, and saw the company of all ages, classes and ranks, on horse and on foot, some joyful and others sad, pass along. Amongst them he distinguished a woman in a meretricious dress, who, from the tenuity of her garments, seemed almost naked. She rode on a mule; her long hair, which flowed over her shoulders, was bound with a golden fillet; and in her hand was a golden rod with which she directed her mule. In the close of the procession a tall, majestic figure appeared in a chariot adorned with emeralds and pearls, who fiercely asked the young man what he did there. He presented the letter in silence, which the demon dared not refuse. As soon as he had read, lifting up his hands to heaven, he exclaimed: "Almighty God!

how long wilt Thou endure the iniquities of the sorcerer Palumbus ! " and immediately despatched some of his attendants, who, with much difficulty, extorted the ring from Venus and restored it to its owner, whose infernal banns were thus dissolved. This legend was made the foundation of Liddell's poem, *The Vampire Bride.*

Dion Boucicault wrote and produced a vampire play entitled *The Phantom,* the scene of which was laid in the ruins of Raby Castle. Anyone remaining in these ruins for one night met with certain death before the morning. The only sign of violence to be found was a wound on the right side of the throat, but no blood was to be seen. The face of the victim was white and the gaze fixed, as though the person had died from fright.

In April 1819 a story entitled " The Vampyre " appeared in *Colburn's New Monthly Magazine,* which was attributed to Lord Byron, but which was really from the pen of Dr John William Polidori (uncle of William Michael Rossetti), who was for a time Lord Byron's travelling physician. The work was also published separately,

13

but the authorship was denied by Lord Byron. Polidori immediately claimed responsibility for the work, and the correspondence and statement of facts published in Rossetti's *Diary of Doctor John William Polydori* show how the mistake occurred.

The following poem appears in the *Life of James Clerk Maxwell*, by Lewis Campbell and William Garnett, and was written by Maxwell in 1845, when he was fourteen years of age :—

THE VAMPYRE

COMPYLT INTO MEETER BY JAMES CLERK MAXWELL

> Thair is a knichte rydis through the wood,
>   And a douchty knichte is hee.
> And sure hee is on a message sent,
>   He rydis sae hastilie.
> Hee passit the aik, and hee passit the birk,
>   And hee passit monie a tre,
> Bot plesant to him was the saugh sae slim,
>   For beneath it hee did see
> The boniest ladye that ever hee saw,
>   Scho was sae schyn and fair.
> And thair scho sat, beneath the saugh,
>   Kaiming hir gowden hair.
> And then the knichte—" Oh ladye brichte,
>   What chance has broucht you here ?
> But say the word, and ye schall gang
>   Back to your kindred dear."

Then up and spok the ladye fair—
    " I have nae friends or kin,
Bot in a little boat I live,
    Amidst the waves' loud din."
Then answered thus the douchty knichte—
    " I'll follow you through all,
For gin ye bee in a littel boat,
    The world to it seemis small."
They goed through the wood, and through the wood,
    To the end of the wood they came :
And when they came to the end of the wood
    They saw the salt sea faem.
And then they saw the wee, wee boat,
    That daunced on the top of the wave,
And first got in the ladye fair,
    And then the knichte sae brave.
They got into the wee, wee boat,
    And rowed wi' a' their micht ;
When the knichte sae brave, he turnit about,
    And lookit at the ladye bricht ;
He lookit at her bonnie cheik,
    And hee lookit at hir twa bricht eyne,
Bot hir rosie cheik growe ghaistly pale,
    And schoe seymit as scho deid had been.
The fause, fause knichte growe pale wi' frichte,
    And his hair rose up on end,
For gane-by days cam to his mynde,
    And his former luve he kenned.
Then spake the ladye—" Thou, fause knichte,
    Hast done to me much ill,
Thou didst forsake me long ago,
    Bot I am constant still ;
For though I ligg in the woods sae cald,
    At rest I canna bee

> Until I sucks the gude lyfe blude
>   Of the man that gart me dee."
> Hee saw hir lipps were wet wi' blude,
>   And hee saw hir lufelesse eyne,
> And loud hee cry'd, " Get frae my syde,
>   Thou vampyr corps encleane ! "
> Bot no, hee is in hir magic boat,
>   And on the wyde, wyde sea ;
> And the vampyr suckis his gude lyfe blude,
>   Sho suckis hym till hee dee.
> So now beware, whoe'er you are,
>   That walkis in this lone wood :
> Beware of that deceitfull spright,
>   The ghaist that suckis the blude.

Mr Reginald Hodder, in *The Vampire*
(William Rider & Son, Ltd.), has developed
a theory which is a novel one in the annals
of vampirism.   The principal character is a
living woman, a member of a secret sisterhood,
who is forced to exercise her powers as a vampire to prevent loss of vitality.   This power,
however, is exercised through the medium of
a metallic talisman, and the main thread of
the story turns on the struggle for the possession of this talisman.   It is wrested ultimately
from the hands of those who would use it for
malignant purposes, but its recovery is only
accomplished by means of a number of
extraordinary—though who would dare say
impossible ?—occult phenomena.

CHAPTER XIII

FACT OR FICTION ?

WHILE some writers, belonging mainly to what is popularly known as the orthodox school of theology or professing a materialistic philosophy, have expressed an entire disbelief in the alleged phenomena, others, on the other hand, accepting generally the spiritistic or spiritualistic philosophy, have admitted their possibility, though not pledging themselves to the acceptance of all or any of the many stories told concerning the deeds, or rather misdeeds, of the apparitions.

Dr Pierart, the well-known French *savant*, maintained that " the facts of vampirism are as well attested by inquiries made as are the facts of catalepsy," and that " the facts of vampirism are as old as the world," and pointed to the fact that Tertullian and St Augustine spoke of them.

Gabriele D'Annunzio was another firm believer in their existence. In his *Triumph of Death*, translated by Georgina Harding, we read : "What have they not done ? Candia told of all the different means they had tried, all the exorcisms they had resorted to. The priest had come and, after covering the child's head with the end of his stole, had repeated verses from the Gospel. The mother had hung up a wax cross, blessed on Ascension Day, over a door, and had sprinkled the hinges with holy water and repeated the Creed three times in a loud voice ; she had tied up a handful of salt in a piece of linen and hung it round the neck of her dying child. The father had ' done the seven nights '—that is, for seven nights he had waited in the dark behind a lighted lantern, attentive to the slightest sound, ready to catch and grapple with the vampire. A single prick with the pin sufficed to make her visible to the human eye. But the seven nights' watch had been fruitless, for the child wasted away and grew more hopelessly feeble from hour to hour. At last, in despair, the father had consulted with a wizard, by whose advice he had called a dog and put the body behind the door. The vampire could not then enter the house till she counted every hair on its body."

Calmet's explanation of the spectres so much talked of in Hungary, Moravia, Poland, and elsewhere is that they are nothing but persons that are still alive in their graves, though without motion or respiration; and that the freshness and ruddy colour of their blood, the flexibility of their limbs, and their crying out when their hearts were run through with a stick, or their heads cut off, were demonstrative proofs of their being still alive. " But this," he says, " does not affect the principal difficulty at which I stick, namely, how they come out of and go into their graves, without leaving any mark of the earth's being removed; and how they appear to carry former clothes. If they are not really dead, why do they return to their graves again and not stay in the land of the living ? Why do they suck the blood of their relations, and torment and pester persons that should naturally be true to them and never give them any offence ? On the other hand, if it be nothing but a mere whim of the persons infested, whence comes it that

these carcases are found in their graves
uncorrupted, full of blood, with their limbs
pliant and flexible, and their feet dirty,
the next day after they have been patrol-
ling about and frightening the neighbourhood, whilst nothing of this sort can be
discovered in other carcases that were
buried at the same time and in the same
mound ?   Whence is it that they come no
more after they are burned or impaled ? "

This is the view accepted by Dr Herbert
Mayo.   He holds that vampires are the
bodies of persons who have been buried
alive, and whose life, where it yet lin-
gered, was finally extinguished through the
ignorance and barbarity of those who
disinterred them.   The Germans express
this condition of the living body by the
term *Scheintod*, which means " apparent
death," which is, perhaps, a better term
than the English " suspended animation " ;
but Dr Mayo, finding both terms in-
adequate, employs the expression " death-
trance."   He regards this trance as a posi-
tive status—a period of repose—the duration
of which is sometimes definite and pre-deter-
mined, though unknown.   But, he continues :

" We have yet to explain the vampire

visit and its consequence, the lapse of the
party visited into death-trance. There
are two ways of dealing with this knot :
one is to tie it, the other to untie it. It
may be cut, by denying the supposed
connection between the vampire visit and
the supervention of death-trance in the
second party. Nor is the explanation thus
obtained devoid of plausibility. There is
no reason why death-trance should not,
in certain seasons and places, be epidemic.
Then the persons most liable to it would
be those of weak and irritable nervous
systems. Again, a first effect of the epidemic might be further to shake the nerves
of weaker subjects. These are exactly
the persons who are likely to be infected
with imaginary terrors, and to dream,
or even to fancy, they have seen Mr or
Mrs Such-a-one, the last victims of the
epidemic. The dream or impression upon
the senses might again recur, and the sicken-
ing patient have already talked of it to his
neighbours, before he himself was seized with
death-trance. On this supposition the vampire visit would sink into the subordinate
rank of a mere premonitory symptom.

"To myself, I must confess this explanation, the best I am yet in a position to offer, appears barren and jejune, and not at all to do justice to the force and frequency, or, as tradition represents the matter, the universality of the vampire visit as a precursor of the victim's fate. Imagine how strong must have been the conviction of the reality of the apparition, how common a feature it must have been, to have led to the laying down of the unnatural and repulsive process customarily followed at the vampire's grave, as the regular and proper preventative of ulterior consequences.

" I am disposed, therefore, rather to try and untie this knot, and with that object to wait, hoping that something may turn up in the progress of these inquiries to assist me in its solution. In the meantime, I would beg leave to consider this second half of the problem a compound phenomenon, the solution of the two parts of which may not emerge simultaneously. The vampire visit is one thing ; its presumed effect another.

" The vampire visit ! Well, it is clear the vampire could never leave his grave bodily —or, at all events, if he could, he never could have buried himself again. Yet in his grave they always found him, so the body could not have been the visitant. Then, in popular language, it was the ghost of the vampire that haunted its future victim." Two instances of the death-trance are quoted.

Cardinal Espinosa, prime minister under Philip the Second of Spain, died, as it was supposed, after a short illness. His rank entitled him to be embalmed. Accordingly, the body was opened for that purpose. The lungs and heart had just been brought into view, when the latter was seen to beat. The cardinal, awakening at the fatal moment, had still strength enough left to seize with his hand the knife of the anatomist.

On the 23rd of September 1763, the Abbé Prévost, the French novelist and compiler of travels, was seized with a fit in the forest of Chantilly. The body was found and conveyed to the residence of the nearest clergyman. It was supposed that death had taken place through apoplexy. But the local authorities, desiring to be satisfied of the fact, ordered the body to be examined. During the process the poor Abbé uttered a cry of agony. It was too late.

Among Theosophists and Continental spiritists a solution to the problem is found in their teaching concerning the astral body and the astral plane, as conveyed by Madame Blavatsky in *Isis Unveiled.*

It is held that so long as the astral form is not entirely separated from the body there is a liability that it may be forced by magnetic attraction to re-enter it. Sometimes it will be only half-way out when the corpse, which presents the appearance of death, is buried.   In such cases the astral body voluntarily re-enters the mortal frame, and then one of two things happens—either the unhappy victim will writhe in the agonising torture of suffocation, or if he has been grossly material he becomes a vampire.   It is held that this ethereal form can go wherever it pleases, and that it is possible for this astral body to feed on human victims and carry the sustenance to the corpus lying within the tomb by means of an invisible cord of connection, the nature of which is at present unknown; but psychical researchers—and these number many eminent scientists—have of late years devoted their efforts towards the elucidation of the phenomenon known as the projection of the double; and this, if scientifically and satisfactorily explained, will give the clue to many of the phenomena of vampirism.

This " double " may sometimes during life be projected unconsciously, and sometimes purposely, by means of hypnotism or provoked somnambulism. An example of the former appeared in the *Journal du Magnétisme* for October 1909, and the translation of the account was published in the *Annals of Psychical Science* for January–March 1910, and is here reproduced. The narrator is M. Antonio Salazar of Mexico.

" *A Romantic Case of Projection of the Double*

" In 1889 I lived at Juatlahuaca, in the state of Oaxaca, Mexico. For a long time I passionately loved the woman who afterwards became my wife.

" At the beginning of 1890, through one of those unfortunate disagreements which occasionally arise between parents and their children, those of my beloved one, wishing to put an end to our mutual love, separated us by taking her to the mountains ; but this only increased our love, because of the difficulties and our desire to see each other.

" Several months passed after our separation, and though the distance between us was not great, we had to take into account

the vigilance with which she was surrounded,
and which was a greater obstacle than the
difficulties of the road.

"One night, when I was feeling, as usual,
very sad and gloomy, the thought came to
me to say to my servant : 'Jeanette, if
any morning you come into my room and
do not find me, do not look for me ; take the
keys and open the shop. If at midday I
have not arrived, you can seek for me in
the mountains.'

"'Ah, sir,' she replied, 'I would never
oppose myself to your commands, if what
you tell me did not concern persons whom
I love and respect, because you will never
thereby accomplish your object.'

"I knew that she was right, and I thought
that the best thing I could do was to go to
sleep and try to calm my imagination.
She also retired, much distressed, and im-
ploring all the saints, to whom she prayed,
to prevent any unfortunate incident which
would threaten the lives of three persons—
my *fiancée*, her father, and myself.

"The following day I awoke with the
same project in my mind, but before carrying
it out I wished to inform my *fiancée* as to
the day and hour at which I hoped to speak

to her. She replied by showing me the
rashness of my project, and offering to do
all she could to overcome the obstacles
which prevented her from returning to live
in the town, which she hoped to do in a
few days, and which came to pass as she
had predicted. I reckoned, however, on
my sagacity and youthful ardour to realise
my project before my *fiancée* was able to
return.

"One day, when my mind was indulging
itself in all kinds of fancies, I thought it
would be quite easy to elude the vigilance
of all those who were around my *fiancée*,
and who were opposed to our meeting.
When night came on I continued to think of
my project, and I resolved to lie down and
try to sleep.

"I passed a very disturbed night, waking
frequently, and when the day began to
break, the servant came to my room to bid
me 'good morning,' and to ask for the
keys of the shop.

"'How have you passed the night, sir ?'
she asked.

"'Rather badly, Jeanette. I have
dreamed continually, and it is impossible
for me to give you an idea of all the dangers

and precipices which I thought I overcame
and crossed ; it seems to me that I went
over the mountain road which leads to the
farm, but it was a very different road.   I
dreamed that our interview was prevented,
I do not know how, and that I had a long
walk home again.   What can it all mean ? '

" ' It is only the result of your wishes
and preoccupation in regard to the young
lady. She will soon return, and then
these follies will disappear.'

" I very soon forgot all about what I have
just described, and so did my servant, for
neither of us attached any importance to a
dream ; but, after a short time, a messenger
from the farm handed me a letter, in which
my *fiancée* reproached me for my violence,
my bad conduct and disobedience in going
there in defiance of the commands and
wishes of her father.

" ' What ?   I ?   No.   Never ! Tell your
mistress that, although I have thought of
going to see her, I have never carried out
my desires ; if I have not done so, it has
not been through lack of courage and will
on my part, but only because of my desire
to please her and not to oppose her wishes.'

" ' But we saw you.'

" ' Me ? '

" ' Yes, sir—you.'

" ' You are telling an untruth. I have not been out. My servant can corroborate that ; and, further, I have nothing to lose by telling the truth.'

" ' That may be as you please, but it is true that you spoke to me ; you questioned me on the subject of Mademoiselle—desired me to tell her that you were there and wished to speak to her.'

" ' These are illusions on your part ; you have been dreaming.'

" ' That is possible ; but there were two, three, all the servants, who also saw you. You did not arrive until nearly midnight ; you were dressed as you are now, and riding a white horse, which you fastened to the gnarled oak. We could all recognise you by the moonlight, and you were going towards the side door when I stopped you from entering.

" ' Hearing our voices, the dogs began to bark, which caused all the servants to get up. You were recognised by my master and the young lady, who fell on her knees before her father, beseeching him not to fire on you. Without showing any fear,

14

you returned step by step to your horse and went down the mountain again. My master was much annoyed with you, called his confidential servant Marino, ordered him to follow you and not to be afraid, but to fire on you two or three times, as he would be responsible. Marino set out, and, although he walked quickly and tried all he could to catch you up, he could not do so. A curious phenomenon aroused his attention, which was that he always saw you going at the same pace, and he had not the courage to fire his rifle.

" ' You arrived at the entrance to the town about five o'clock in the morning; the moon was setting and the day commencing to break. Before you arrived at the first crossing of the streets you began to run, and turned quickly along the first street in the town; and though Marino ran after you, he lost sight of you at the next crossing.'

" My persecutor, frightened by what he had seen, returned immediately to the farm to inform his master of what had taken place, and which seemed very extra-ordinary and supernormal.

" For a long time this adventure, of which

I was the unconscious hero, made a great stir in the town."

Colonel de Rochas, a distinguished French savant, has made this question of the externalisation or projection of the double and of the motricity and sensibility of the subject his special and patient study, and has embodied the results of many of his experiments in separate works. Some have also been published in the pages of the *Annals of Psychical Science,* so that the reader who is particularly interested in the question will have no difficulty in finding material for further consideration and study.

The Société Magnétique de France has also conducted extensive experiments in this field of research, particulars of which are published from time to time in the *Journal du Magnétisme.* The following theoretical explanation given at the conclusion of the report of a series of these experiments is reprinted from the *Annals* for July–September 1910 :—

" We know that the phantom is the psychical body projected from the physical body. It is that which enjoys or suffers, thinks, wishes, judges, and perceives all sensations. It is constantly animated by extremely rapid vibratory movements which are certainly the same as when it is within the body. This principle being admitted, we understand that, when it animates the body, its vibratory movements are not projected outside, and that it exercises no appreciable action on other organisms in its neighbourhood. But when it is outside the body its movements are easily externalised. Then the phantom and another person, vibrating in unison, represent two stringed instruments which sound at the same time when one only is touched. If this transmission can be effected at great distances, we can explain this strange and unexpected phenomenon by the theory of wireless telegraphy or telephony."

The results of the many experiments conducted by and under the auspices of French scientists in particular tend to indicate that in the near future an explanation of the phenomena of vampirism will be forthcoming.

In 1733 there was published a small work entitled *Philosophicæ et Christianæ Cogitationes de Vampiriis,* by Joanne Christophoro Herenbergio. The author speaks of

a spectre which appeared to him in full
daylight ; at the same time he submits
that vampires are not the living dead,
and that everything that happens can
be debited or should be attributed to
the disturbed imagination of the sick. He
demonstrates, by various experiments, that
imagination is capable of causing great
disturbances in the body and dispositions.
He recalls that in Sclavonia they impale
murderers, and that they pierce the hearts
of the guilty with a stake. If they make
use of the same punishment against vampires it is because they look upon them
as the authors of the death of those whose
blood they are supposed to suck. Chris-
topher Herenberg, to Anglicise his name,
gives two illustrations of this punishment,
one of the year 1337, and another in 1347 ;
he also makes reference to the opinions of
those who believe that the dead eat in
their tombs, the antiquity of which opinion
he proves from Tertullian, by a quotation
from his work on the Resurrection, and by a
reference to St Augustine, Book viii., *City
of God*. The quotation from Tertullian
proves beyond doubt that the pagans
offered nourishment to their dead, even

to those whose bodies had been burned, in the belief that their souls would feed on it. This had reference, however, not only to the pagans, for St Augustine speaks in several places of the Christian custom, particularly in Africa, of bringing meat and wine to the tombs, when there was a devotional feast to which the relatives and friends of the deceased were invited, as well as the poor. In course of time this feasting was prohibited.

In certain parts the soil seems to be favourable for the preservation of dead bodies in all the freshness of life. At Toulouse, in the vault of a monastic chapel, in 1789, some bodies were found to be perfectly whole, and they resembled living people, although they had been interred for close on two centuries. The bodies were ranged around the wall, still wearing the vestments in which they had been buried. The phenomenon was the more singular as, on examining, two or three days after-wards, the bodies interred on the opposite side of the chapel, they were found to be crumbled away.

Calmet reports one particular instance, when in villages alleged to be infested with vampires, the authorities went to the cemeteries and inspected the graves. Wherever there were found two or three or more holes about the size of a finger in a grave it invariably contained a supple and ruddy body. If the head of this corpse were cut off there always came from the arteries abundant fresh fluid blood. The question was then asked by the Benedictines whether such holes could contribute to the preservation of life and render more credible the story of the return of the dead to the living, but the conjecture is not deemed by Calmet worthy of attention. The same writer also quotes elsewhere a letter from M. De l'Isle de Saint-Michel, who lived for a long time in the infested country of Hungary, and who made a lengthy study of the subject. His letter is as follows :—

" A person is found attacked with languor, loss of appetite, grows perceptibly thinner, and at the end of eight or ten days, sometimes fifteen, dies without fever or any other symptom of disease. Then, in Hungary, they say that a vampire has become attached to him and has sucked his blood.

" Of those who are attacked with this

foul melancholy, the majority, having a disturbed mind, believe that they see a white spectre which follows them always like the shadow made by the body.

" When we were on duty in the winter among the Valaques, two troopers in the company of which I was cornet died of this malady, and several others who were attacked would probably have died if a corporal of the company had not dispelled their fears by making use of a remedy which the men of that country employed for that purpose. Although very singular, I have never read of it in any ritual. It is as follows :—

" They choose a young boy, who must be of an age to be pure in body, that is to say one whom they believe to be a virgin. They make him ride barebacked on an absolutely black horse, also a virgin. They lead the boy and the horse to the cemetery and make them walk on all the graves. Any one which the animal refuses to pass, despite the blows of the horsewhip which are delivered, is regarded as holding the body of a vampire. The grave is opened, and they find within a beautiful and fresh body as of a man sleeping tranquilly.

They cut with one blow of the spade the neck of this corpse, an abundance of fresh, red blood shoots forth ; at least they claim to see it. This done, the vampire is replaced in the grave, which is filled in, and they believe that from that moment the attack ceases, and that those who were attacked recover their strength gradually, as men emerging from a long, exhausting illness."

An extraordinary idea adopted in some villages is that the moon reanimates vampires. This opinion occurs in Polidori's novel *The Vampyre*, wrongly attributed to Lord Byron. Ruthven, killed by brigands, asked that he might be exposed to the rays of the moon, and, after a quarter of an hour, he was reanimated.

BIBLIOGRAPHY

Abercromby's *Finns.*
Arabian Nights' Entertainments.
Leo Allatius.
Barth's *The Religions of India.*
Bartholin's *de Causa contemptûs mortis.*
Beaumont's *Treatise on Spirits.*
Blavatsky's *Isis Unveiled.*
John Brompton's *Chronicles.*
Calmet's *Dissertation upon Apparitions.*
Calmet's *The Phantom World.*
Caylus's *Contes Orientaux.*
Charlemagne's *Capitularies.*
Hugh Clifford's *In Court and Kampong.*
Codrington's *Melanesians.*
Conway's *Demonology and Folk-lore.*
William Crooke's *Popular Religion and Folk-lore of Northern India.*
Gabriele D'Annunzio's *The Triumph of Death.*
Hector de Boethius's *History of Scotland.*
Debonnair's *Histoire de France.*
De Schartz, *Magia Postuma.*
C. M. Doughty's *Arabia Deserta.*
Eaves' *Modern Vampirism.*
Encyclopædia Britannica.
E. P. Evans's *Criminal Prosecution and Capital Punishment of Animals.*
Eyre's *Discoveries in Central Australia.*
Farrer's *Primitive Manners and Customs.*
Fornari's *History of Sorcerers.*
Fortis' *Travels in Dalmatia.*
Frazer's *Golden Bough.*
Georget's *Examen Médical des Procès Criminels.*
Goethe's *Bride of Corinth.*
Baring Gould's *Book of Were Wolves.*
Grimm's *Teutonic Mythology.*
J. J. Morgan de Groot's *Religious System of China.*
Baron von Haxthausen's *Transcaucasia.*
Herenberg's *Philosophicæ et Christianæ Cogitationes de Vampiriis.*
Hikayat Abdullah.
Reginald Hodder's *The Vampire.*

Jewish Encyclopædia.

Keightley's *Fairy Mythology.*

T. S. Knowlson's *Origin of Popular Superstitions.*

Leake's *Travels in Northern Greece.*

Liddell's *The Vampire Bride.*

Mackenzie and Irby's *Travels in the Slavonic Provinces of Turkey in Europe.*

Mayo's *On the Truths contained in Popular Superstitions.*

J. A. Middleton's *Another Grey Ghost Book.*

Minstrelsy of the Scottish Border (vol. ii.).

More's *Antidote against Atheism.*

Nider's *Formicarius.*

Laurence Oliphant's *Scientific Religion.*

Pashley's *Crete* (vol. ii.).

Phlegon's *Fragments.*

Polidori's *The Vampyre.*

Michael Psellus' *Dialogus de Operationibus Dæmonum.*

Ralston's *Russian Folk Tales.*

Ralston's *Songs of the Russian People.*

Nicolas Ramy's *Demonolatrie.*

Sutherland Rattray's *Ashanti Proverbs.*

Philip Rehrius's *De masticatione mortuorum in tumulis.*

Roussel's *Transfusion of Human Blood.*

Rycaut's *The Present State of the Greek and Armenian Churches.*

Rymer's *Varney the Vampire.*

St Augustine's *City of God.*

St Clair and Brophy's *Bulgaria.*

Saxo Grammaticus' *Danish History.*

Sayce's *Ancient Empires of the East.*

Scoffern's *Stray Leaves of Science and Folk-lore.*

Sir Walter Scott's translation of *Eyrbyggia Saga.*

Siegbert's *Chronicle.*

W. W. Skeat's *Malay Magic.*

Skeat and Blagden's *Pagan Races of the Malay Peninsula.*

Southey's *Thalaba the Destroyer.*

Bram Stoker's *Dracula.*

R. Campbell Thompson's *The Devils and Evil Spirits of Babylonia.*

J. Pitton de Tournefort's *A Voyage into the Levant.*

Tozer's *Researches in the Highlands of Turkey.*

Trumbull's *Blood Covenant.*

Turner's *Nineteen Years in Polynesia.*

Tylor's *Primitive Culture.*
Voltaire's *Dictionnaire Philosophique.*
Horace Walpole's *Reminiscences.*
Westermarck's *Origin and Development of Moral Ideas.*
William of Newbury.

ARE ANY OF THESE IN A DATABASE?

PERIODICAL LITERATURE

All the Year Round (vol. xxv.).
Annals of Psychical Science.
Blackwood's Magazine (vol. lxi.).
Borderland.
Chambers's Journal (vol. lxxiii.).
Colburn's Magazine (vol. vii.).
Contemporary Review (July 1885).
Gentleman's Magazine (July 1851).
Household Words (vol. xi.).
Journal du Magnétisme.
Journal Indian Archipelago (vol. i.).
Journal of Psychological Medicine.
Lippincott's Magazine (vol. xlvii.).
London Journal (March 1732).
New Monthly Magazine (1st April 1819).
Nineteenth Century (September 1885).
Notes and Queries.
Occult Review.
Open Court (vol. vii.).
Revue Spiritualiste (vol. iv.).
St James's Magazine (vol. x.).
Wonderful Magazine (1764).

PRINTED IN GREAT BRITAIN BY NEILL AND CO., LTD., EDINBURGH.